Must-See Japan

**The most complete insider guide to seeing
the best of Japan in one short trip**

By Tom Fay

Must-See Japan

The complete insider's guide to seeing the best of Japan in one trip

About the author

Tom Fay is a British author and freelance writer who has been living in Japan for almost a decade. He has written extensively about the outdoors and travel in Japan, both online and in print, for The Guardian, Forbes Travel Guide, Japan Today and many other media outlets.

He has a keen interest in landscape photography, and is the main author of the forthcoming guidebook 'Walking and Trekking in the Japan Alps' to be published by Cicerone Press. See (www.thomasfay.com) for examples of his work and for contact information.

Contents

Kamikochi, in the Japan Alps

A snowy shrine entrance in Zao, Yamagata Prefecture

1. Introduction

Japan is a beautiful, multi-layered and often perplexing country. There is so much for the visitor to enjoy; sprawling mega-cities, unspoilt wilderness, history and tradition at every turn, ultra-modern technology, old fashioned charm, abundant natural wonders, numerous world heritage sites, bullet trains, top quality cuisine, world class shopping and service, the list is almost endless. But all of this variety, all of these places and the limitless choices on offer, can make planning and executing a trip to Japan somewhat overwhelming. Where are the best areas to visit? What is a truly authentic Japanese experience? How can I feel like I've 'done' Japan? For travellers with a limited amount of time, questions such as these can cause all sorts of headaches. There is so much on offer in Japan, so much to see and do, that it can be hard to plan an itinerary without trawling through countless guidebooks and searching the internet for hours on end.

That is where this guidebook comes in. With close to a decade's worth of experience of living in the country, and having helped any number of family members, friends and acquaintances during their trips to Japan, I will point you to the best, absolute must-see places, many of them famous, some of them off the usual tourist radar, but all easily accessible using public transport and most importantly, each one showing the best that Japan has to offer. Visitors usually want to visit the most famous sights and eat the must-try foods, but it's also worth getting off the main tourist trail to uncover a side of Japan that most people rarely get to see. Indeed, some of the most memorable travel experiences are often of that sort; discovering a quiet corner of a Shinto shrine, trying to converse with friendly and curious locals, wandering down some dimly-lit backstreet only to find the best ramen shop this side of Fukuoka.

The problem is, such experiences can be hard to stumble across if you don't know where you should be looking, and as is often the case when on a short trip abroad, it's possible to get so burnt out trying to see absolutely everything, that smaller, but ultimately more memorable experiences can pass right under your nose. This guide has all the practical information to help you use your time wisely. It will tell you the things you simply must not miss, with all of the big hitters included (if they merit it of course). But along the way, there will be suggestions for slightly off-the-beaten-track places of interest, visits to which will allow you to get under the skin of this complex yet enthralling, and totally unique country.

This is not a completely exhaustive guide to every tourist spot in the country, or even to all of those in the main cities. In a country where the streets often have no names and even the locals don't always know how to read the *kanji* place names, the best way to navigate these days is by using a smartphone or tablet (see chapter 14 for details on using Wi-Fi in Japan). For more old-fashioned travellers, tourist information centres in the bigger train stations often provide paper maps for free.

Simply consider the suggestions in this guidebook, visit the places that pique your interest and have your own adventures. Treat this guide as the trusted, practical advice of an old friend to help you get the most out of your stay. Make your trip to Japan an unforgettable one. Almost everything you need is here.

The magnificent Todai-ji in Nara

2. Planning your itinerary

Visitors to Japan come from all over the world, and stay for varying lengths of time. As there is so much to see and do, it can be a logistical nightmare trying to plan a balanced itinerary that offers a little taste of everything, without missing anything out. For visitors on long trips, where time is less of an issue, planning where to go and what to do can be a more leisurely affair. However for most people, a trip lasting for one or two weeks is fairly typical, but this requires much more stringent planning to make use of the limited time available. People on such tight schedules frequently ask about the best places to visit, how best to get there, and how long to stay in each area. What follows are basic breakdowns of the main targets for a week-long or a two week trip; if you have more time to play with then all the better!

Obviously it is impossible to see all of the country in such a short space of time, so included here are the key places which simply cannot be missed, leaving time for a few less well-known, but equally memorable side-trips. Chapter 9 has some further suggestions for interesting places to visit if time allows, but for now, treat everything in this current section as the very core of your trip. Include all of these places on your itinerary, and you can't go far wrong.

Think of Japan, and most people conjure up images of vast neon metropolises, serviced by quicker-than-a-flash bullet trains, and this is a world that certainly exists to an extent. Tokyo/Yokohama, Nagoya, Osaka and Kobe are all ultra-modern mega cities, and a visit to at least one of them is essential. However, there is so much more to Japan than these concrete playgrounds, and you are not seeing the real Japan unless you escape the urban sprawl and sample the slower pace of life in the countryside, where often it seems that time has stood relatively still.

Most visitors to Japan arrive at Narita International Airport on the outskirts of Tokyo, but the older Haneda Airport also serves the capital, and other international hubs include Kansai Airport (Osaka), Nagoya and Fukuoka airports, all of which are also served by many of the big international airlines. Wherever you arrive, the following same information applies, just amend your arrival and departure points. Also, don't forget to buy a JR Rail Pass before you arrive in Japan (*see Chapter 13*), an investment which is well worth making if you intend to city-hop or travel around the country a bit.

If you have about a week in Japan, then you will want to be spending at least two nights in Tokyo, as this should give you just enough time to see most of the main sights (albeit briefly). You may then have the opportunity to spend a night in one of the popular weekend getaways for busy Tokyoites, such as picturesque Hakone or Nikko. This can be followed by another night near one of the scenic lakes at the foot of the iconic Mt. Fuji. After that, it's a short ride on the bullet train for the 3 hour journey to the Kansai area, home to the cultural capital Kyoto, historic Nara and the culinary metropolis of Osaka, any one of which makes for a good base to explore the area. Aim to spend two or three nights in the region, before heading to Kansai Airport (or back to one of Tokyo's airports) and flying home.

This short itinerary allows you to sample both the eastern (*Kanto*) and western (*Kansai*) regions of the country and gives you a good taste of modern city life, as well as the chance to experience the slower pace and beauty of rural Japan; what's more, you'll be able to see many of Japan's most well-known sights and it should make for a fantastic, balanced trip (see the later chapters for much more detailed information).

One week itinerary:

Tokyo (Kanto) area (3 days)
↓
Mt. Fuji area (1 or 2 days)
↓
Kyoto (Kansai) area (3 days)

If your trip is for two weeks or so then you will be able to spend more time exploring the above areas, as well as adding a few more side-trips.

Two week itinerary:

Tokyo (3 or 4 days)
↓
Tokyo side-trip eg. Hakone, Oze, Nikko
(2 or 3 days)
↓
Mt. Fuji area (2 days)
↓
Kyoto (3 days)
↓
Kansai day-trips eg. Osaka, Nara (2 days)
↓
Other side-trips eg. Koya-san, Hiroshima
(1 or 2 days)

Following the above itinerary will give you ample time in both Tokyo and Kyoto to see all of the main sights without feeling rushed, as well as allowing you to explore various areas outside of the main cities. Indeed it is often said that you won't see the real Japan unless you leave the big cities and sample Japan's wonderful nature and countryside, and this itinerary allows for that.

Include a night or two in a *ryokan* (a traditional Japanese hotel, *see chapter 18*) for the complete 'Japan' experience.

Kyoto's historic Higashiyama district

3. Using this guide

This guide serves as a list of recommendations of what to see and do in the three main, must-see areas; Tokyo (Kanto), the Mt. Fuji region and Kyoto (Kansai). It has been quite a challenge to decide what to include, but all of the recommendations in this book come from years of accumulated travel experience, whether it be my own trips around the country, or various trips made by trusted friends and acquaintances. With the purchase of a JR Pass it is possible to make great use of the public transport system in Japan to see many places, even in a short period of time.

Every place named in **bold** type is well worth a visit and should be considered if your time allows.

Places with a **double asterisk (**)** after their names are pretty much essential and can be considered absolutely 'must-see'.

Following every suggestion in this book would realistically take at least three weeks or thereabouts. So if you have less time than that, try to include all of the places with an asterisk to their name, as well as a selection of the regular bold recommendations. This will make for a varied, balanced trip, including enough famous sights to feel like you have 'done' Japan (although it goes without saying there remains a lot more to be discovered).

Chapter 9 serves as a brief introduction to other areas of the country, either for those with more time on their hands, or for further trips in the future.

Be sure to check the later chapters of the guidebook for food and restaurant recommendations, hotel and accommodation suggestions, and lots of other useful and practical information to help make your trip go smoothly.

Symbols - Throughout the guidebook you will see the following symbols which denote the following:

◙ - web address

☼ - opening hours

¥ - price or entry (in yen)

351-0043 - post code (use to search for an address).

Note* Japanese addresses can be notoriously difficult to decipher, even for Japanese people, and the post code may only direct you to the general area, so it's always best to check online beforehand for a precise location.

Insider tips:

Look out for these at the end of each section; they will point you towards some particularly interesting or possibly lesser known sights, include unique personal tips or advice, or reveal a local recommendation not typically listed in the guidebooks.

A snowy scene in the Japanese countryside

4. Must-see Tokyo

The bustling and endlessly sprawling capital city of Japan, Tokyo is one of the great cities of the world and is usually the first stop for most people visiting the country. Its 23 wards are home to a population of 9 million people, and as part of the wider Greater Tokyo region, makes up the world's largest metropolitan area with close to 38 million people living there. It is no surprise then that there is a lot to see and do in Tokyo, with its ultramodern skyscrapers, historic shrines, peaceful parks and gardens, fashionable shopping districts and a world-class culinary scene (more Michelin star restaurants than any other city on earth).

Despite Tokyo's intimidating size, many of the most popular and famous areas are located on or near the JR Yamanote line, which loops around central Tokyo. Some of the main stations include Shinjuku, Shibuya, Ikebukuro, Akihabara, Tokyo and Shinagawa (the latter two also serving the Kyoto-bound *Tokaido shinkansen*). Thirteen subway lines crisscross most of central Tokyo (they are not covered with the JR Pass), but English signage and announcements are good, so it's fairly easy to get around. Aim to book a hotel anywhere along or within the loop of the Yamanote line and you'll have good access to all of the sights.

Getting there – Narita International airport is Tokyo's main airport (the other being Haneda), and it is located about an hour away from the city in the rather rural and neighbouring Chiba prefecture. There are two main ways to reach Tokyo from Narita; by bus or by train (or taxi if you are super rich!).

Please see 'Chapter 12: *Getting to and from the airport'*, for much more detailed information on this.

Insider tip:

- If you plan on using your JR Pass straight away then you can activate it at Narita, but if you plan on staying in Tokyo for a few days at first, then it may be worthwhile investing in a Pasmo or Suica card (see Chapter 13) from the JR ticket office; they are top-up cards for use on all trains, subways, buses and even in some shops (costs 500 yen for the card plus the amount you wish to charge it with).

Central Tokyo

In a city that's as large and brimming with variety as Tokyo is, it can be hard to pin-down the absolute must see sights. However, if you only have two or three days in the city, then the following places are all interesting and well worth trying to squeeze into your schedule.

Shinjuku area **

Shinjuku is one of the 23 city wards in Tokyo, and as well as being an administrative and commercial centre for the city, it is also a hub for entertainment and shopping, and is also home to the busiest railway station in the world (Shinjuku station). As well as having plenty of points of interest in its own right, its central location and abundance of hotel options makes it a good place to stay whilst in Tokyo.

If you can escape the throngs of people and slightly disorientating layout of Shinjuku station, a quick 10 minute stroll to the west will lead you to the **Shinjuku skyscraper district**. It is home to some of Tokyo's tallest buildings and most famous hotels (including the Park Hyatt from *Lost In Translation*), but the main recommendation here would be the **Tokyo Metropolitan Government Building**, whose 243 metre high twin towers each have free observatories on the 45th floors. The southern tower is said to have slightly more interesting views.
(◙ www.metro.tokyo.jp/ENGLISH/OFFICES/ observat.htm ☼ 9.30am-11pm ¥ free)

Just a five minute walk northeast of Shinjuku station is **Kabukicho**, one of Tokyo's largest and unashamedly seedy entertainment districts. There are countless restaurants, bars, love hotels and shifty looking touts on street corners just looking to exploit naive tourists. Although Japan is an extremely safe country, this is one of the few areas where you should use just a bit of common sense, and it is best to just ignore the touts. One of the main attractions in Kabukicho is the **Golden Gai**, a district full of narrow, claustrophobic streets which come alive at night, the many tiny bars and hole-in-the-wall eateries only having room for a handful of customers. If Japanese is not your forte be on the look out for places with English signs and menus out front.

Directly northwest of Shinjuku station is **Omoide Yokocho**, or otherwise endearingly nicknamed *Piss Alley*, a rabbit warren of alleyways next to the railway tracks which is home to a variety of tiny and cheap counter restaurants serving *yakitori, ramen* and *soba* noodles. On the opposite side of Shinjuku station (to the south) is the newly developed **Southern Terrace** where you can find slightly fancier department stores, restaurants and cafes.

The last Shinjuku recommendation is **Shinjuku Gyoen National Garden** (200 yen entrance fee), a ten minute walk east from Shinjuku station's 'New South Exit'. It is one of the largest and most historic parks in Tokyo, and is a wonderful escape from the bustle of the city, with its perfectly manicured Japanese and English gardens, green and scenic areas, and various varieties of cherry blossom trees (meaning a better chance to see some in bloom). Visit in late November or December for the stunning autumn colours.

You could easily spend a whole day (or longer) discovering the delights of Shinjuku, but if you are on a tight schedule, a full afternoon and an evening should allow you just enough time to see some of the main sights.

Insider tips:

- Not a typically touristy thing to do, but if you are around Shinjuku station between 7.30am and 8.30am on a weekday, try to find a quiet corner among the throngs of commuters silently passing in all directions; the mass of people and hypnotic sound of thousands of echoing footsteps makes for a unique and somewhat surreal 'only in Japan' experience.

- The wealth of establishments in the Golden Gai means choosing a place to drink at can be difficult. For an authentic experience (cheap drinks, non-stop karaoke and a smoky atmosphere) head to **One Coin Bar Champion** in the southern part of the Golden Gai, it's very popular with locals (160-0021).

- Check out the **Samurai Museum** in Kabukicho; excellent displays and some cool live demonstrations.
(◉ www.samuraimuseum.jp/en/ ☼ 10.30am-9pm, ¥1800 adult/¥800 child, 160-0021)

Shibuya and Harajuku **

The Shibuya area is one of Tokyo's liveliest and busiest districts, where fashion, youth culture, shopping and entertainment all meld into one. Directly outside of Shibuya station's Hachiko exit is the world famous **Shibuya Crossing****, reputed to be the world's busiest pedestrian crossing. Across the road from the station are a multitude of shops and department stores, including Shibuya 109 (young girls' fashion), Tokyu Hands (interior, stationary, and hobby), Seibu and Parco (both fashion). The **Center Gai** is the unmissable busy pedestrian street in the heart of Shibuya, lined with shops, neon signs and cool young people just hanging out.

Slightly to the north is the **Koen Dori**, a pleasantly wide and popular shopping street which leads all the way to **Yoyogi Park**, one of Tokyo's largest and most spacious green areas. The park is good fun to wander around (particularly at weekends) when 50s style rockers congregate for dance-offs, and it is a great spot for people watching.

Right next to the park is **Meiji Shrine****, an impressive shrine complex dedicated to the deified spirits of Emperor Meiji. The entrance to the shrine is through a huge torii gate, from where the path winds through a surprisingly deep and serene forest (considering this is in the middle of Tokyo) before reaching the shrine buildings. The Treasure House and Inner Gardens each cost 500 yen to enter, but the main shrine is free. Yoyogi Park and the Meiji Shrine are both easily accessed from Harajuku station on the Yamanote line.

Harajuku** itself is Tokyo's youth culture capital, focused on the Takeshita Dori (east from the station), a narrow street lined with quirky shops and often even quirkier fashions. At the end of the street, head south (turn right) and you will discover the swanky **Omotesando** district, a broad tree-lined avenue (Tokyo's answer to the *Champs-Elysees*) full of brand name shops and a more upmarket clientele.
Omotesando Hills is a fancy shopping complex with interesting architecture, while just down the street you can find Kiddy Land, one of Tokyo's best toy stores.
(◉ www.omotesandohills.com/english
☼ 11am-10.30pm)

Harajuku and Shibuya can both be seen in half a day of pleasant strolling, starting at either Harajuku or Shibuya JR stations and ending at the other one.

Insider tips:

- Fans of the 2003 movie *Lost In Translation* should head to **Karaoke-Kan** in Shibuya (150-0042, *30-8 Utagawacho*), it's the karaoke bar which Bill Murray and Scarlett Johansson visit.

- **Fujiya Honten** (☼ 5pm-11pm/closed sundays, 150-0031) is a great, slightly old-style standing bar/izakaya close to Shibuya, delicious food and drink at dirt cheap prices.

- Head to Harajuku on Sunday afternoons to see groups of cosplayers milling about, while over in Yoyogi Park 50s style rockers dance and jive away.

- Harajuku may be the youth culture capital, but Shimokitazawa is like its cooler, more secretive sibling; second-hand clothes shops and stores selling records and retro items line the narrow alleys, while interesting music venues and bars await discovery. It's not actually that close to Harajuku however; take the Keio Inokashira line from Shibuya, or the Odakyu line from Shinjuku.

Ginza and Imperial Palace **

If Omotesando whet your appetite for upmarket chic, then **Ginza** will be like heaven. This area has some of the priciest real-estate in the world

(1sqm of land estimated at over ten million yen!) and so is naturally full of premium brand shops and expensive restaurants. The main **Chuo Dori** street is closed to road traffic on weekend afternoons, and so this is a good time to stroll around and smell the luxury. The most famous landmark is Ginza Wako; the legendary building with its famous clock tower on the Chuo street corner. Nearby is the Sony Building, where all the latest products are showcased to the public, and there are numerous department stores at almost every turn.

For a spot of culture, head to the **Kabukiza Theatre** to catch a performance of this traditional theatre where language is not always so much of a barrier (even native speakers often struggle with the antiquated Japanese used), as the story is mostly conveyed through actions. Tickets start from 4000 yen.
(◙ www.kabuki-bito.jp/eng/top.html
¥4000-20,000, 104-0061)

Ginza is easily accessed from JR Yurakucho station, or Ginza station if using the subway.

A little north of Ginza is one of Tokyo's most famous landmarks, the **Imperial Palace**. While the inner grounds of the palace are not usually open to the public, the Imperial Palace East Gardens contain wide lawns, the impressive remains of the former Edo Castle and a lovely

Japanese garden. They are closed on most Mondays and Fridays however.
(◉ www.kunaicho.go.jp/event/higashigyoen/ gyoen-close.html) for the monthly calendar.

The Imperial Palace is a ten minute walk west from the Marunouchi side of **Tokyo Station**, which has been impressively restored to its pre-war condition.
Both Ginza and the Imperial Palace can easily be visited in half a day.

Insider tips:

- On Ginza's Chuo street, lookout for a shop called **Ito-ya**; easily recognisable by the huge red paperclip hanging above the entrance. This flagship store is arguably the best place to shop for Japanese stationary in the whole of Tokyo.

- The **Hamarikyu Gardens** are a somewhat hidden gem close to Ginza, peaceful and pretty parkland in the heart of the city with seawater ponds and a wonderful teahouse serving *macha* (green tea).
(◉ www.teien.tokyo-park.or.jp/en/hama-rikyu/ ☼ 9am-5pm, ¥300, 104-0046)

Akihabara **

Known by *otaku* (diehard fans) throughout the world, Akihabara is the anime, videogame and cosplay capital of Japan. It can be busy and overwhelming, but is a very 'Japanese' experience. This relatively compact area has a high concentration of electronics stores, including well known giants such as Yodabashi Camera, Sofmap, Laox and Yamada Denki, as well as countless anime emporiums, retro videogame shops and collectible stores.

Maid cafes are also popular, as dainty young girls in French maid outfits serve tea and engage in chitchat with customers.
Head to **@Home Café** for English speaking maids and afternoon tea and snacks.
(◙ www.cafe-athome.com/en ☼ 10.30am-10pm, 101-0021)

For aficionados, Akihabara offers days of entertainment, but for most people an hour or so is more than enough. Akihabara station is on the JR Yamanote line.

Insider tip:

- Videogame fans should head to Super Potato, a huge store crammed with retro games and goodies. Hidden away on the top floor is an arcade featuring countless retro classics.

Asakusa **

One of the few districts where the Tokyo of the past seems to live on, Asakusa should be included on most itineraries. Despite being bombed heavily during the Second World War, Asakusa retains its sense of history, with the 7th century **Sensoji** arguably being Tokyo's most famous temple. It can be reached by walking up the always bustling Nakamise shopping street from the equally well-known **Kaminari Gate**, a local landmark with its huge red lantern. The gate (and the nearby uniquely-designed tourist information centre) are just a stone's throw away from Asakusa subway station.

Twenty minutes walk away from Asakusa across the Sumida River is Tokyo's newest landmark, the **Tokyo Skytree** which at 634m is Japan's tallest structure. There are two observation decks, tickets for the lower one being 2060 yen, while the higher deck tickets are an additional 1030 yen. Foreigners who show their passports at a separate ticket counter can buy a slightly more expensive 'Skytree fast ticket' to skip the waiting lines. There are often waiting times of well over an hour to access the observation decks, and combined with the fairly high ticket prices, a trip to the top is probably not essential. The Skytree is often lit up at night, when it is best viewed from a distance (the Sumida River being a good spot).

(◙ www.tokyo-skytree.jp/en ☼ 8am-10pm, ¥ from 2060 yen, 131-0045)

The closest stations to the Skytree are Tokyo Skytree station on the Tobu Isesaki line, and Oshiage station on the Asakusa, Hanzomon and Keisei Oshiage lines.

Insider tips:

- Fans of *tempura* (items fried in a light batter) should head to **Sansada** in Asakusa, reputed to be the first restaurant in Japan to serve *ten-don*, a rice bowl topped with *tempura*.
(☼ 5pm-9pm weekdays / 11.15am-3pm and 5pm-9pm Saturdays /closed Sundays, ¥850-2500, 111-0032)

- Another historic, but less well-known area is the **Yanaka district** just north of Ueno Park. The old *shitamachi* atmosphere from Tokyo of yesteryear still survives here; the streets are full of rustic charm, busy locals and a whole variety of shops and trades. There are now very few places in Tokyo quite like it, and its well off the usual tourist trail. The Yanaka Cemetery is also nicely landscaped and worth a visit.
Yanaka Ginza (the main shopping street) is an eight minute walk west from Nippori station on the Yamanote line.

Roppongi

Formerly known as the district for raucous nightlife, Roppongi has a more sophisticated side to it these days following the development of a number of museums, luxury hotels and elegant retail and residential projects. That's not to say that the nightlife went anywhere though, as the streets just south of Roppongi station are still full of foreigner-friendly bars, clubs and restaurants, all popular with the local expat community, if sometimes a little on the seedy side.

To the west is **Roppongi Hills**, a stylish complex of office and residential spaces, shops and restaurants, and the Mori Art Museum and Tokyo City View Observation deck, which offers possibly the best views of the city from anywhere in Tokyo (if a little pricey at 1800 yen).
(◉ www.roppongihills.com/tcv/en ☼ 10am-11pm, ¥1800 adult/¥600 child, 106-6108)

Just a little north is the **National Art Centre**, a magnificent venue which hosts a range of temporary exhibitions.
(◉ www.nact.jp/english ☼ 10am-6pm/closed Tuesdays, 106-8558)

Heading back east, the **Tokyo Midtown** complex is also an impressive sight, especially the Midtown Tower, which at 248m is one of the tallest buildings in Tokyo and is home to the Carlton-Ritz, one of the city's nicest hotels. The complex also houses the Suntory Museum of Art and a range of stylish restaurants and shops. (◉ www.tokyo-midtown.com/en ☼11am-12pm, 107-0052)

Roppongi station is best reached on the Hibiya and Oedo subway lines, or from Roppongi-Icchome station on the Nanboku subway line.

Insider tips:

- Roppongi has a reputation as a seedy and somewhat dangerous place (especially among Japanese people), and by Japanese standards it probably is! However, if you take the same precautions as you would on a night out in any other big city around the world then you won't have any problems. Just ignore any street touts who may approach you.

- Just north of Roppongi in Akasaka there is a well hidden (as might be expected!), but popular ninja-themed restaurant called **Ninja Akasaka**, featuring a ninja-inspired menu, interesting décor and surprise events. (◉ www.ninjaakasaka.com ☼5pm-1am, 100-0014)

Tsukiji fish market

One of the biggest fish markets in the world, a visit to see the early morning tuna auctions has become something of a holy grail for many visitors to the capital, despite the fact that this is a busy working market and only 120 tourists are admitted every day.

If you wish to see the auction, head to the Osakana Fukyu Centre at the Kachidoki Gate of the market from around 5am, as entry is on a strictly first come first served basis. The first group of 60 will be admitted to the inner market between 5.25 and 5.50am, while the second group can enter from 5.50 to 6.15am. There are often queues long before 5am however, and there are strict rules which must be followed when inside.

For a more leisurely experience, head to the outer market where there are a number of stalls and tiny hole-in-the-wall restaurants serving up the freshest sushi for breakfast. Most of these close around noon, and the most popular establishments (such as Sushi Dai) can have 2 or 3 hour waiting times!

Tsukijii fish market was due to move location to Toyosu in early 2017, but this move has now been postponed indefinitely (although you should check online for any new updates).

(◙ www.tsukiji-market.or.jp/tukiji_e.htm ☼ 5am-1pm / closed sundays, national holidays, 2nd and 4th wednesdays, and around New Year, 104-0045)

The market can be accessed directly from Tsukiji Shijo subway station, or it's a five minute walk from Tsukiji station on the Hibiya subway line. For JR Pass holders it's a 15 minute walk from JR Shimbashi station.

Insider tip:

- Head to **Iwasa Sushi** and order the chef's *omakase* set; incredible sushi and nothing like the long waits at the more famous establishments such as Sushi Dai or Daiwa. (◙ www.iwasasushi.com/en ☼ 6am-2.30pm / closed sundays, public holidays and wednesdays when the market is closed too, ¥1000-4000, 104-0045)

Odaiba

Built on a manmade island in Tokyo Bay, Odaiba has a fresh, modern feel, with many interesting buildings and pleasant open spaces. It has become a popular date spot, with many choices of shops, restaurants and entertainment options to while away an afternoon or evening.
The futuristic looking **Fuji TV Building** is the headquarters of one of Japan's biggest TV

stations, and nearby **Decks** is a shopping mall with lots on offer including Tokyo Joypolis, Legoland Discovery Centre and Madam Tussauds wax museum.
(◙ www.odaiba-decks.com/en
☼ 11am-11pm/shops, restaurants and attractions vary, 135-0091)

DiverCity Tokyo Plaza is a relatively new shopping complex with a huge Gundam statue standing outside.
(◙ www.divercity-tokyo.com/en/ ☼ 10am-11pm, 135-0064)

Palette Town is another large shopping centre, housing attractions such the European-styled Venus Fort shopping area, an enormous ferris wheel and Leisureland, where you can enjoy bowling, karaoke, arcade games and some sports.

Odaiba is connected to Tokyo by the Rainbow Bridge (which can be walked across in 35 minutes), and taking the elevated Yurikamome train (not JR Pass valid) from Shimbashi on the JR Yamanote line (15 minutes, 320 yen). This train ride is an experience in itself, offering fantastic views out over Tokyo Bay. It is also possible to take the Rinkai line to either Tokyo Teleport or Kokusai Tenjijo stations, but the JR Pass is not valid here either.
There are also boats from Asakusa (50 minutes, 1560 yen) for a more unique approach.

Insider tips:

- Part of the Palette Town complex is the Toyota Mega Web, which is a must-see for anyone into cars (you can even test drive some new models). The History Garage showcases many old models from a variety of manufacturers in a range of settings, interesting for even non-petrol heads.

- Avoid the Sewage Museum; not even interesting in a quirky kind of way, it's just dull.

Edo-Tokyo Museum

Located in an interesting looking building in the Ryogoku district (famous for *Sumo* wrestling), this fascinating museum shows what Tokyo would have looked like during the Edo period, with many lifelike models and figurines on display.

Between 10am and 3pm English-speaking volunteers are on hand to explain some of the details, and there are a number of temporary Tokyo-related exhibits too. Entry is 600 yen, and it can be reached in about five minutes from JR Ryogoku station.
(◙ www.edo-tokyo-museum.or.jp/en/ ☼ 9.30am-5.30pm / closed mondays or the following day if monday is a national holiday, ¥600, 130-0015)

5. Must-do daytrips from Tokyo

Although Tokyo and its outlying areas seem to spread out in one huge, concrete jumble as far as the eye can see, you only need to hop on the train for a relatively short time to escape the city and experience another side of Japan completely. The following day trips and half-day trips are all easy to do from central Tokyo, and it would certainly be worth trying to fit at least one of them into your itinerary.

Tokyo Disneyland is only about 40 minutes from central Tokyo by train, but its popularity and sheer size means that you need more than a day there to enjoy it fully. Note that it's also possible to visit the Mt. Fuji area as a day trip from Tokyo, but Chapter 6 covers the region in greater detail.

Kamakura **

One of the most popular day trips from Tokyo, and for good reason. Kamakura is known as the *Kyoto of Kanto* (the eastern region of Japan) and as such is home to a wealth of historical and cultural sights. This small city was the seat of the military government which ruled Japan from 1192 until political power moved to Kyoto in the 14th century. Kamakura's most famous landmark is the **Great Buddha**, a 13 metre tall statue cast of bronze in 1252 and part of the Kotokuin Temple complex. It was originally housed in a wooden building, but that was destroyed by typhoons and tsunamis, and so since 1495 it has been sitting out in the open air. Entry to the temple is 200 yen, and it is located 8 minutes walk away from Hase station on the Enoden line (this is a streetcar style train line whose main terminal is next to JR Kamakura station).

Just five minutes walk from Hase station is **Hasedera** (Hase Temple), one of the many popular temples in Kamakura. This one is famous for its eleven-headed, 9.1 metre high wooden statue of Kannon, the goddess of mercy. The grounds also contain pretty gardens and a small museum, and there a good views over Kamakura city. Entry is 300 yen.
(◙ www.hasedera.jp/en/ ☼ 8am-5pm (Mar-Sept), 8am-4.40pm (Oct-Feb), ¥300, 248-0016)

The impressive **Tsurugaoka Hachimangu** is Kamakura's most important shrine, and it has a long, wide approach all the way from the waterfront, right through the city centre, passing under multiple red torii gates on the way. Many events take place throughout the year (New Year is particularly special and busy), and entry to the shrine is free. It can be reached in 10 minutes by walking from Kamakura station down the Komachi-dori shopping street, or by taking the Dankazura, a cherry tree-lined pedestrian street (connected to Wakamiya Oji Street).
(◙ www.tsurugaoka-hachimangu.jp ☼ 6am-8.30pm, ¥ Free, 248-8588)

41

Just west of Kamakura is **Enoshima**, a pleasant, touristy island with a few shrines, parks, caves and an observation tower. It can be reached by taking the Enoden line all the way to its terminus at Enoshima station (25 minutes, 260 yen). Nearby there is also an aquarium and a number of beaches, which being some of the closest sandy beaches to Tokyo are very popular in the summer.

Getting there: Kamakura station is about an hour away from Tokyo, with a choice of JR services including a direct train from Tokyo station (60 minutes, 920 yen).

Insider tip:

- If looking to take a break, head to **Itsuki Garden**. Located in the grounds of a private residence, hikers would often get lost when walking the nearby trail to Kamakura's giant Buddha, but the garden's friendly owner offered them tea and a place to rest. Gradually he built outdoor brick terraces where guests could relax and enjoy the beauty of the forest, making for quite a unique and serene café experience. (◙ www.itsuki-garden.com/en ☼ 10am-6pm closed Tuesdays, 248-0022)

Nikko **

This is a small town on the edge of Nikko
National Park, an area full of scenic mountains,
lakes, hot springs, wild monkeys and which is
crisscrossed by numerous hiking trails. The town
itself has been the centre of Buddhist and Shinto
mountain worship for centuries, and so is full of
temples, shrines and a deep sense of history. It
makes for a nice escape from the city, and can
be done as a daytrip (although a night staying in
a *ryokan* is highly recommended).

Toshogu Shrine is a lavish complex, functioning
as the mausoleum of Tokugawa Ieyasu, the
founder of the *shogunate* which ruled over Japan
for over 250 years until the Meiji Restoration in
1868. The shrine contains a mix of Shinto and
Buddhist elements, and it is rare to see such a
luxuriously decorated shrine anywhere in the
country. Admission to all parts of the shrine is
1300 yen, and it can be reached by bus (10
minutes, 310 yen) or by a 30 minute walk from
JR Nikko station.
(◙ www.toshogu.jp/english ☼ 8am-5pm Apr-Oct /
8am-4pm Nov-Mar, ¥1300, 321-1431)

There are many other interesting shrines in the
town, but for a pleasant half hour stroll, the
Kanmangafuchi Abyss cannot be beaten. This
gorge was formed following the eruption of
nearby Mt. Nantai and an easy riverside walking
trail has been built, lined with about seventy

stone *Jizo* statues. The walk can be accessed by taking a Tobu bus bound for Chuzenjiko Onsen or Yumoto Onsen and getting off at Tamozawa bus stop (10 minutes from JR Nikko, 310 yen). Alternatively, it is a 30 minute walk from Toshogu Shrine.

If you have more time (two or three days ideally) it is great to explore the **Okunikko** area, a mountainous region inside Nikko National Park which offers fantastic natural scenery. Highlights include **Lake Chuzenji** at the foot of Mt. Nantai, and the nearby **Mt. Hangetsuyama**, where easy hiking trails (or a bus) lead to great views of the surrounding landscape. **Kegon Waterfall** is one of Japan's three most beautiful waterfalls and is accessible from Chuzenjiko Onsen bus terminal (50 minutes from JR Nikko station, 1150 yen). Slightly further northeast is the **Senjogahara Marshland**, where boardwalks and hiking trails can be easily followed (with snowshoeing possible in winter), and further north again is **Yumoto Onsen**, an idyllic hot spring town full of *ryokans* (80 minutes by Tobu bus from Nikko, 1700 yen).

Getting there: Nikko can be reached from Tokyo using JR or Tobu railway lines. For JR Pass holders, it's easiest to take the Tohoku *shinkansen* to Utsunomiya station and then changing to the JR Nikko line (100 minutes).

The Tobu line starts at Tobu Asakusa station, from where trains depart for Tobu Nikko (120 minutes, 1360 yen).
There are 2-day unlimited passes for Tobu buses and trains, which includes trains from Tokyo to Nikko.
Check (◙ www.tobu.co.jp/foreign/en) for details.

Yokohama

The second largest city in Japan, and only a short distance from Tokyo, Yokohama is a major port of historic and commercial importance. Down by the waterfront, **Yamashita Park** is a public park with lots of open, green spaces. Next to the promenade is an impressive ocean liner called the **Hikawa Maru**. This retired ship from the 1930s served the imperial royal family and celebrities such as Charlie Chaplin travelling first-class between Yokohama and Seattle, and now functions as a museum (entry 300 yen, closed Mondays). The park is a five minute walk from Motomachi-Chukagai station on the Minato Mirai line.

Next to Yamashita Park is **Osanbashi Pier**, the terminal where international cruise ships dock when in Yokohama, and the area has many pleasant walkways and green spaces, as well as fantastic views of the **Minato Mirai** skyline. Meaning 'harbour of the future', the Minato Mirai district is full of high-rise buildings, shops, hotels, an amusement park, museums (including the cup noodle museum), hot springs and parks, all in a lovely waterfront location. It can be accessed from Minato Mirai station on the Minato Mirai line, or from Sakuragicho station on the JR Negishi line (one stop from Yokohama).

To get a sense of Yokohama's history, head to the hilly **Yamate** area where a number of foreign residences from the early 20th century have been well preserved (Japan's isolationist policy was ended in the 1850s and this area was one of the first to open up to foreign traders). Admission to most of the houses is free. At the foot of the hills is the **Motomachi** shopping street, where designer brand shops and fashionable cafes all vie for attention. The nearest station is Motomachi-Chukagai (8 minutes, 210 yen from Yokohama station) on the Minato Mirai line or Ishikawacho (7 minutes, 160 yen) on the JR Negishi line. The Yamate district is within walking distance, or you can catch a bus (¥220) on the 'Akaikutsu' loop.
(◉ www.yokohama-bus.jp/akaikutsu/en/index.html)

Just east of Motomachi is Japan's largest **Chinatown**, which is full of colourful Chinese gates and slightly 'Japanified' restaurants and food stalls. The closest stations are Motomachi-Chukagai and Ishikawacho.

Getting there: There are regular trains from Tokyo to Yokohama (25 minutes, 470 yen) on the JR Tokaido line.

Hakone

A popular weekend retreat for busy Tokyoites, Hakone is famous for its hot springs, abundant natural beauty and great views of Mt. Fuji. Check (◙ www.hakone.or.jp/en) or (◙ www.hakonenavi.jp/english) for good information on attractions, hot springs and accommodation in Hakone.

The hot springs are what bring most people to the area, and **Hakone Yumoto** is the most famous hot spring resort (15 minutes from Odawara on the Hakone Tozan Railway, 310 yen), and easily doable as a day trip from Tokyo.

There are a large number of quality bathhouses and *ryokan* to choose from including **Kappa Tengoku** with its outdoor baths on a wooded slope, and convenient location close to the station. (◙ www.kappa1059.co.jp/index.html ☼ 10am-10pm, ¥800, 250-0311)

The clean and new indoor, outdoor and private baths at **Hakone Yuryo** are also worth investigating.

(◙ www.hakoneyuryo.jp/english ☼ 10am-9pm /
weekends open until 10pm, ¥1400 adults/¥700
children, 250-0315)

Tenzan is in the classic style, with its beautiful
outdoor pools and traditional style building
(website is all Japanese, so for more details ask
at Yumoto tourist information centre).
(◙ www.tenzan.jp ☼ 11am-8pm, ¥1100
adults/¥650 children, 250-0312)

Most of the attractions in Hakone are centred
around Mt. Hikone and **Lake Ashinoko**. Some
of the best views of the lake (with Mt. Fuji in the
distance) are from Moto-Hakone, a small town
on the southern end of the lake, from where it is
possible to take boat cruises to the northern side.
(takes about 30 minutes, ¥1000, ◙ www.hakone-
kankosen.co.jp/foreign/en for details)

There are frequent buses between Odawara
station and Moto-Hakone (50 minutes, 1180 yen),
but it is worthwhile purchasing a Hakone Free
Pass to allow unlimited travel on Hakone Tozan
buses. The pass can also be used on the
Hakone Tozan Railway, a slow but scenic
approach to the northern end of the lake.
(◙ www.hakone-tozan.co.jp/en, ¥620 max)

The Hakone Free Pass site (◙ www.odakyu.jp/
english/deels/freepass/hakone) has lots of
information.

Hakone Shrine is located on the shores of Lake Ashi and lies hidden in the forest with its path marked by lanterns and torii gates, creating an otherworldly ambience, particularly when it is misty. It is a five minute walk from Moto-Hakone boat pier. There is another shrine on the top of Komagatake, one of Mt. Hakone's sacred peaks, which can be reached by taking the Komagatake Ropeway from Hakone-en.

Owakudani is a crater area where sulphurous gases escape from the ground, hot springs bubble and even the rivers are heated. There are a number of short walking trails in the area, accessed from Owakudani station on the Hakone Ropeway. However at the time of writing, the ropeway from Sounzan is closed due to increased volcanic activity. The ropeway between Togendai and Owakudani is open, but visitors cannot leave Owakudani station.

Getting there: From Tokyo take the *shinkansen* to Odawara station (35 minutes, 3740 yen), or a train on the JR Tokaido line (80 minutes, 1490 yen).

Kusatsu

Another famous hot spring resort, Kusatsu is located high up in the mountains of Gunma prefecture, with waters said to heal every ailment apart from lovesickness. In the centre of the town you can find the intriguing **Yubatake** (hot water field), a sulphur-smelling 70 degree Celsius hot spring pumping out over 5000 litres of water per minute, which is then distributed to all the bathhouses in town via a series of wooden channels. People wearing *yukata* mill about in the evenings, and there is a free foot spa (*ashiyu*) to use, as well as various shops and *ryokan* around the Yubatake's perimeter.

There are a number of free community bathhouses dotted around the town too, which typically are gender segregated and only accommodate two to four people. Larger, more famous bathhouses include **Gozanoyu**, an attractive wooden building next to the Yubatake (500 yen), **Otakinoyu**; outdoor baths and indoor wooden pools of varying water temperatures (800 yen), and **Sainokawara Rotemburo** with its large outdoor pools and adjacent walking paths among a landscape of warm streams and heated waterfalls (600 yen). Sainokawara Park is worth visiting even if you don't enter the baths and is just a ten minute walk northwest from the Yubatake.

Getting there: Take a JR train from Tokyo or Ueno stations to Naganohara- Kusatsuguchi station (160 minutes, 6000 yen) and then a JR bus to Kusatsu Onsen (30 minutes, 690 yen). Of course, both the train and bus are free for JR Pass holders. It is also possible to take the *shinkansen* to Takasaki and then transferring to a local train, but it only saves about 30 minutes.

Mt. Takao

If you are pushed for time, but want to escape the city for half a day, then Mt. Takao (599m) is a good option. The mountain is located inside Tokyo metropolitan area, and has a number of easy hiking trails, of which Trail No. 1 is the easiest and quickest (mostly paved, 90 minutes to the summit). The other trails are a bit longer, unpaved and quieter, and all eventually reach the same place. There is also a short cable car and a chair lift to make the ascent even easier (both 480 yen one way). There are a number of things to see along the way, including the attractive **Yakuoin** temple near the summit, and a monkey park and wild flower garden (420 yen). On a clear day you can see out to Mt. Fuji, while the mountain is particularly popular in the autumn (so avoid weekends to dodge the crowds).

Getting there: Take the JR Chuo line from Shinjuku to Takao station (40 minutes, 550 yen) and then transfer to the Keio line for one stop to Takaosanguchi station (3 minutes, 130 yen). Alternatively a direct semi-limited express train from Keio Shinjuku takes about 50 minutes (390 yen, JR Pass not valid). There is a nice hot spring bathhouse behind Takaosanguchi station.

Oze

A unique national park with lots of great scenery and easy hiking, Oze is famous for its marshlands and blooming white skunk cabbages (prettier than they sound!). With an early start it is certainly possible as a daytrip from Tokyo, although if time allows, a night in a nearby *ryokan* or mountain hut will allow for a more leisurely pace.

There are a number of easy and flat trails to the **Ozegahara Marshland**; picturesque any time of year but especially when the skunk cabbages bloom in May and June, or when the yellow alpine lilies flower in the summer. About a 90 minute walk through forest to the east is **Ozenuma Pond**, well know for its abundant wildflowers.

A hike to either the marshland or the pond can easily be done as a day trip (both about 4 or 5 hour roundtrips), but a full loop taking in all the sights will take closer to 9 hours, so it is better to stay in one of the mountain huts which are dotted around. See (◉ www.oze-fnd.or.jp/en) for a little information about the area.

Getting there: For the popular Hatomachitoge trailhead which leads to the marshland you can take the *shinkansen* to Jomo Kogen station (75 minutes, 5500 yen), and then take a bus to

Tokura (110 minutes, 2450 yen), from where there is a short shuttle bus to the trailhead. For the Oshimizu trailhead (which is closest to Ozenmua Pond) do the same as above but take a bus for Oshimizu instead of Tokura. Alternatively, take the *shinkansen* to Takasaki and transfer to a local train for Numata station. From there, there are numerous buses to Tokura and Oshhimizu. The JR Pass covers all the trains here.

Zao Fox Village

Located deep in the mountains of Tohoku, in the shadow of the mountain of the same name, the **Zao Fox Village** is a unique attraction where visitors can get up close and personal with a surprisingly large variety of these furry and cute creatures. The foxes freely roam around a spacious preserve, and many of the tame ones will happily scamper up to visitors, looking for food (which can be bought for 100 yen). There is also a miniature petting zoo on site, featuring rabbits, goats and other animals, and all in all, it makes for a rather charming and memorable experience. Entry is 1000 yen per person, children under 12 are free!
If visiting in winter, wrap up warm and bring sturdy footwear as it can be very snowy from December through to April.
(◉ www.zao-fox-village.com/en ☼ 9am-4pm, ¥1000, 989-0733)

Despite being quite a distance from Tokyo (Sendai is the nearest big city), Zao Fox Village is possible as a day trip from the capital, and is certainly worth the effort if you have a JR rail pass and a day to spare. The surrounding countryside is also quite beautiful, and nearby Mt. Zao is an interesting and popular hike around a volcanic crater in the summer, with plenty of skiing options in the winter.

Getting there: It can be a little awkward to visit, but the easiest way from Tokyo is to take the *shinkansen* to Shiroishizao (109 minutes, 10,350 yen) and get a taxi (20 minutes, 4000 yen, can take a bit longer in winter on icy roads) to the fox village. The friendly tourist information office at the station can help with calling a taxi.

It's also possible to take the *shinkansen* to Fukushima and then change to a local train as far as Shiroishi station (135 minutes, 9600 yen). From there you can take a 20 minute taxi ride (around 4000 yen) to the village, or there is a much cheaper, but very infrequent bus (1 hour, 200 yen), which departs in the morning, needs booking in advance and doesn't always run, so can't be relied upon.

Alternatively, if you fancy exploring the area a little further and in your own time, it may be worthwhile renting a car from Fukushima instead.

6. Must-see Mt. Fuji

While it's possible to visit the Mt. Fuji area as a daytrip from Tokyo, it's much more rewarding to spend a little more time there, and so it's recommended to stay at least one night in any of the villages or towns lying in the shadow of the iconic mountain. Mt. Fuji itself, at 3776m high, is the tallest mountain in Japan; snow capped for roughly half the year and it is easy to forget that it is actually an active volcano. Luckily it hasn't erupted since 1708, and so is currently climbable during the brief climbing season (see *Climbing Mt. Fuji* later in this chapter for details). However, with its almost perfectly symmetrical cone, Mt. Fuji has been a mountain revered through the ages, and is arguably better viewed from afar than climbed itself. The area surrounding Mt. Fuji (particularly to the north and east) is known as the Fuji Five Lakes region (*Fujigoko*) and is dotted with picturesque lakes and numerous hot springs, and it makes for a fabulous destination in between city-hopping from Tokyo to Kyoto.

Getting there – It's easy to travel from Tokyo to the Fuji Five Lakes region; a train to Kawaguchiko station takes about 2 hours from Shinjuku station (4110 yen). Note that you must change to the Fujikyu railway line at Otsuki, so your JR Pass won't be valid for the later section of the journey.
Use (◉ www.hyperdia.com) to check train times and connections.

55

Alternatively there are numerous buses from Tokyo and other locations, see (◙ www.bus-en.fujikyu.co.jp) for more information.

**Lake Kawaguchiko **

There are five main lakes at the base of Mt. Fuji, but Kawaguchiko is the most easily accessible and has plenty to see and do. Most people come to this area to catch a glimpse of Mt. Fuji, but as the mountain is often shrouded in cloud a clear view can never be guaranteed (early morning is reputed to offer the best chance). Regardless, the northern shores of the lake have the best viewing spots. Just outside Kawaguchiko station is the **Fuji-kawaguchiko Tourist Information Centre**, which is well worth popping in to obtain free maps of the area and to get suggestions for the best attractions and hot springs to visit. The **Kachi Kachi Ropeway** (720 yen return) takes visitors up to the top of Mt. Tenjo from where you can see all of Lake Kawaguchiko and nearby Mt. Fuji (on a good day). It's also possible to hike back down the mountain in 30 minutes. Just take the bus from Kawaguchiko station to Yuransen Ropeway Iriguchi bus stop, or walk there in 15 minutes.

There are many museums around the lake, the most curious of which is the **Kubota Itchiku Art Museum** on the lake's northern shores. The artist's interesting kimono designs are the main attraction, but the buildings are made from Okinawan coral and limestone, and the gardens take inspiration from African and Asian influences. Entry is 1300 yen, and the nearest bus stop is Kubota Itchiku Bijutsukan.

Lake Kawaguchiko is pleasant to stroll around, and the promenade near **Kawaguchiko Music Forest** (quirky museum devoted to automatic musical instruments, 1500 yen) has some great views of Mt. Fuji, especially during cherry blossom season.

Insider tip:

- Try the local speciality noodles at a branch of **Houtou Fudou**; these udon are bigger and thicker than regular udon, and are served in great big iron pots, making for a very filling and satisfying meal (and they can only be found in the Fuji Five Lakes region).
(◙ www.houtou-fudou.jp/english.html ¥500-1000)

Chureito Pagoda **

For the ultimate 'Japan' photo, head to the **Arakura Sengen Shrine** where you will find the five-storey Chureito Pagoda on the mountainside overlooking Fujiyoshida City and the distant Mt. Fuji. It takes five minutes to walk up the hill from the shrine, but the views are worth it as you can get a quintessential snap of Mt. Fuji with the pagoda in the foreground, and if you visit in mid-April, cherry blossom framing the picture (or autumn leaves in early November).

The shrine is a ten minute walk from Shimo-Yoshida station on the Fujikyu line (10 minutes from Kawaguchiko station, 300 yen, JR Pass not valid).

Fuji-Q Highland

One of Japan's most popular theme parks, **Fuji-Q Highland** offers a dizzying array of record-breaking roller coasters and anime themed rides and attractions. Some of the star attractions include Takabisha (the world's steepest roller coaster with a 121 degree drop), Dodonpa (world record holder for fastest acceleration) and Eejanaika (most inversions on a rollercoaster, includes rotating seats).

If time is tight you can pay 1500 yen to enter the park, and then pay to go on rides individually (typically between 400 and 1000 yen per ride). If you have all day however, an unlimited ride pass costs 5700 yen.
(◉ www.fujiq.jp/en ☼ 9am-5pm/6pm weekends and holidays, ¥1500-5700, 403-0017)

Fuji-Q Highland can be reached from Fujikyu Highland station, just two minutes from Kawaguchiko station on the Fujikyu line (170 yen,

JR Pass not valid). There are also many buses on the Kawaguchiko line.

Hot springs

The area around Mt. Fuji is known for its geothermal activity and so there are abundant hot springs to be enjoyed. Many *ryokan* and hotels have their own baths which are open to non-staying guests. Ask at the tourist information centre for detailed information.

Close to Lake Kawaguchiko and Fuji-Q Highland, **Fujiyama Onsen** is probably the best; a modern version of a traditional wooden bathhouse, with gender separated indoor and outdoor baths. There are no views of Mt. Fuji (apart from at the restaurant) however. Cheapest admission is 620 yen in the mornings, rising to 1250 yen on weekdays and 1550 yen on weekends, and the bus there takes ten minutes from Kawaguchiko station.

Yurari is a modern but beautiful hot spring, with gender segregated indoor and outdoor baths. Second floor baths has great views of Mt. Fuji, and there are private baths (good for couples) available for 1700 yen for 50 minutes. Yurari is close to Lake Saiko and can be reached by taking a Shin-Fuji, Shimobe Onsen or Motosuko-bound local bus from Kawaguchiko station to

Fuji Midorino Kyukamura bust stop (15 minutes, 590 yen).

On the western tip of Lake Yamanakako, **Benifuji-no-yu** doesn't look special from the outside, but its gender separated indoor and outdoor baths have some of the best views of Mt. Fuji among all the hot springs in the area. Benifuji can be reached by taking a Fujikko bus from Fujisan station, while other buses stop at Hananomiyako-Koen bus stop which is just five minutes walk down the road.

Climbing Mt. Fuji

Mt. Fuji (3776m) is a beautiful and iconic mountain which in all honesty, is best viewed from afar rather than climbed itself. However, during the climbing season (early July to early September) thousands of people attempt the hike to the top, and it can get so busy that large queues form along many sections of the trails, with the summit a heaving mass of humanity. Despite its popularity, it is not a mountain to be taken lightly, as the effects of altitude sickness can begin to set in from 2500m, the temperature can be close to freezing near the top (even in the height of summer) and the weather is very prone to change.

Most people start the hike late in the day, sleep for a few hours in one of the mountain huts, and then set off for the summit in the dark to (hopefully) see the sun as it rises in the east. It is always best to make a reservation for a night in a mountain hut (6000 yen to 9000 yen depending if meals are included), and although the huts will often try to squeeze in as many people as possible anyway, it's probably best not to take any chances.

Alternatively, get an early start and climb Mt. Fuji as a day hike (but check the return bus times in advance).

The mountain is split into a number of stages or stations, and there are a multitude of trails and routes to choose from, the most popular being the Yoshida Trail from Fuji Subaru Line 5th Station, which is easily accessible from Kawaguchiko. The ascent from here takes about 5 to 7 hours, (with the descent taking around 3 to 5 hours) but it depends on your fitness and the crowds.

All climbers should be well-equipped (correct footwear, waterproof/warm clothing, sunscreen, water/snacks, flashlight) and should not take the mountain lightly, as even in fine weather it is a long and tiring slog.

It is possible to climb just before or after the climbing season (late June/mid-September), but huts and transport may be limited. Outside of climbing season, Mt. Fuji is a very serious proposition only for those with lots of winter mountaineering experience.

Check (◙ www.fujisan-climb.jp/en) for all the information you need when planning your climb.

Insider tips:

It is possible to climb Mt. Fuji outside of the official climbing season however, and if you want to avoid the crowds then this is the best time to do it.

Aim for a week or two before the official opening on July 1st, or during the first few weeks of September.

Be warned that facilities (i.e. mountain huts) may not be open at that time, and public transport options may be more limited (so renting a car and driving to one of the trailheads may be a good option). Also it is likely to be colder and the weather less stable (rainy season in June and typhoon season in September).

As stated before, climbing Mt. Fuji at any time of year is not to be taken lightly, and if climbing out of season you must take full responsibility for yourself and for those in your party (the local authorities will likely be less sympathetic should something go wrong).

However, if the weather is good and the summit is clear (both of clouds and of people) then climbing Mt. Fuji just outside of climbing season is a truly unforgettable experience.

7. Must-see Kyoto

The Kansai region in western Japan is arguably the historical and cultural heartland of Japan, with the picturesque former capital of Nara and the busy merchant city of Osaka both well worth a visit. However, Kyoto is the star of the show; its perfect Zen gardens, countless temples and shrines, traditional wooden buildings and fleeting glimpses of *geisha* drawing visitors from all over the world.

Kyoto is a relatively compact city, with its streets laid out in a grid pattern, and most visitors will arrive at Kyoto station in the south of the city. Slightly further to the north however is the downtown area around **Shijo**-dori and **Kawaramachi**-dori, and this is where we can find the city's best shopping and entertainment. It's possible to walk here from Kyoto station (takes about 25 minutes), but taking the Karasuma subway line to Shijo-Karasuma station is much quicker.

Just to the east of Kawaramachi is the **Kamo River**, which is pleasant to stroll along whatever the season. Many of Kyoto's most interesting sights are spread out around the edges of the city, and are best reached by a combination of trains and subway or bus.

Public transport in Kyoto can be a little confusing, as there are a number of different (non-JR) train lines, subways and bus routes.
(◉ www2.city.kyoto.lg.jp/koho/eng/access/ transport.html) for public transport information.

Insider tip:

- If staying in Kyoto for a few days it might be worthwhile investing in a top-up Icoca card (available at JR stations), as this can be used on all buses, subways and trains (including non-JR) in the Kansai region.

- Cycling is another good option for getting around Kyoto; there are a number of bike rental shops around the city, prices start at about 1000 yen per day. Ask at the tourist information centre at Kyoto Station for more details.
Also, check (◉ www.cyclekyoto.net) for friendly and interesting bicycle tours.

Getting there – From Tokyo it only takes 140 minutes on the *Tokaido shinkansen* when riding a Nozomi train. Unfortunately JR Pass holders aren't permitted to use the Nozomi, so the next best option is the Hikari, which takes about 160 minutes.
Kyoto is one hour from Osaka's Itami airport (mostly domestic flights), and about an hour and half from Kansai International airport. There are many trains to Osaka from Kansai airport (60 minutes/about 1200 yen) from where it is

possible to get a connection to Kyoto. The JR Limited Express 'Haruka' runs directly from the airport to Kyoto station every 30 mins (2850 yen non-reserved).

There are also frequent airport buses which take about 100 minutes.
(◉ www.okkbus.co.jp/en/timetable/kix/f_kyt.html ¥2550).

Central Kyoto

Kyoto has far too many temples, shrines and interesting places to visit for them all to be mentioned here, so the following locations are simply some of the best, or most iconic ones. See (◉ www.kyoto.travel/en) for comprehensive listings.

If time is short, aim to explore the area east of the Kamo River, where many of Kyoto's most famous historical sites and landmarks are located.

Insider tips:

- Try to branch off from the main tourist trails, and explore the quieter side streets around the main tourist areas; you'll often discover something unique and interesting.

- To avoid the crowds and to really see Kyoto at its atmospheric best, explore the city's historic districts at dawn or dusk.

- Check out **Kyoto Guide**, the useful monthly guide for visitors, readable online.
(◉ www.kyotoguide.com)

Gion and Higashiyama **

The Gion district is the Kyoto of most people's imaginations; traditional wooden teahouses (*ochaya*) lining the narrow streets, with the chance to spot *geisha* and *maiko* (their apprentices) going about their business.
Hanami-Koji Street is the most popular area (south branching street from the main Shijo-dori road, five minutes from the Shijo Bridge), with its expensive restaurants serving *kaiseki ryori* (Japanese haute cuisine) and atmospheric teahouses.

A slightly quieter quarter is the **Shirakawa** area (5 minutes north of the Shijo-dori main street), with its many high-class restaurants overlooking the willow-lined canal. Even if Gion's expensive establishments are well out of your budget (prices start from about 10,000 yen per person), it is a fascinating and evocative district to walk through.

From Gion it is only a short walk east to the **Higashiyama** district, another of Kyoto's best preserved areas. The streets between **Kiyomizudera** and **Yasaka Shrine** (with its 5-storey pagoda) are narrow and winding, and full of traditional merchant's stores which now serve as charming shops and cafes. Kiyomizudera (400 yen) is one of Kyoto's, if not Japan's most famous temples and is well worth a visit. It is possible to explore both Gion and Higashiyama within an hour or so if time is at a premium.

For the energetic, it is possible to extend the walk as far as **Ginkakuji** (the Silver Pavilion) via Nanzen-ji and the Philosopher's Path.

It is easy to walk to Gion from Shijo and Kawaramachi; just cross the bridge over the Kamo River. The nearest station is Gion-Shijo on the Keihan line.

Insider tips:

- **Kenninji Temple** is located right in the heart of Gion, at the southern end of Hanami-Koji street, but despite it being one of Kyoto's most interesting zen temples, many tourists seems to pass it by. It has several nice gardens (including the Circle-Square-Triangle garden, built on the idea that all things in the universe are based on these shapes), lots of fine artwork (including exquisite painted screen doors) and is only 500 yen to enter.

- Easily missed but well worth the effort of going there, **Sanjusangendo** is one of the most spectacular and unique temples in the whole of Japan. Comprising of a 120m long temple hall (the longest wooden structure in Japan), inside of which stand 1001 human-size statues of the goddess of mercy, Kannon. It really is an awesome sight. The temple is a five minute walk from Shichijo station, or a 20 minute walk east from Kyoto station.

- Next door to Sanjusangendo is **Yogen-in**, one of Kyoto's most historically important temples but little visited by tourists. It is home to some amazing paintings and some pretty ghastly (but fascinating) stories, evidence of which can still be seen on some of the wooden ceilings panels, where trails of blood and handprints remain stained in the wood after the ritual suicide of over three hundred soldiers in 1600.

Ginkakuji (Silver Pavilion) and the Philosopher's Path

Not so far from Gion and the Higashiyama districts, **Ginkakuji** is a Zen temple modelled on Kinkakuji (see next section), and although not actually silver in colour it is a structure of exquisite form and beauty. The surrounding sand and moss gardens are pleasant to walk through, and as Ginkakuji is usually a little less busy than its golden equivalent, it can be a somewhat more serene experience. Entry is 500 yen, and it can be reached by taking bus 5, 17 or 100 from Kyoto station (40 minutes, 230 yen).

Alternatively, follow the Philosopher's Path from **Nanzen-ji** Temple. This Zen temple complex is one of the most important in all of Japan, and the grounds are free to wander around with much of interest to see, including the impressive Sanmon Gate and the famous Hojo rock garden (500 yen). The nearest station is Keage on the Tozai line, from where it is a five minute walk north.

It is also worth checking out **Eikando**, a Buddhist temple just north of Nanzen-ji famous for its autumn leaves which are lit up on selected evenings. Entry is 600 yen.
See (◙ www.eikando.or.jp/English/ eikando_e.html) for further information.

The **Philosopher's Path** runs north from Nanzen-ji, and gets its name from a famous philosopher who used to walk the 2km on his daily commute to Kyoto University. The stone path follows a canal lined with cherry trees, and so is one of the most popular places to see the blossom in early April.

Insider tip:

- Visit **Murin-an** (just west of Nanzen-ji), one of Kyoto's most peaceful and beautiful gardens, but often overlooked by tourists.
(◙ www.murin-an.jp/en ☼7.30am-6pm but varies so check website, ¥410)

Kinkakuji (Golden Pavilion) **

One of Japan's most iconic buildings, Kinkakuji was built as the retirement villa of the shogun Ashikaga Yoshimitsu in the early 1400s and became a Zen temple after his death. The top two floors are completely covered in gold leaf, with the surrounding gardens and the building's reflection in the pond combining to make a picture perfect scene. Kinkakuji is well worth visiting, but due to its popularity it can get extremely busy, so perhaps aim to go just before closing time (17:00) to avoid the worst of the crowds. Entry is 400 yen.

Kinkakuji is in the north of Kyoto and is a little awkward to get to. Take bus 101 or 205 from Kyoto station (40 minutes, 230 yen) or alternatively take the subway to Kitaoji station and then a ten minute bus to the temple.

Fushimi-Inari **

This is one of the most unique Shinto shrines in
the whole of Japan, and is most famous for the
thousands of red torii gates which adorn all the
trails weaving up the mountain. Inari is the
Shinto god of rice, and foxes were thought to be
the god's messengers, so keep your eyes
peeled for the fox statues which are dotted
around. The full hike takes about 2 hours, but if
time (or energy) is lacking, then you need only
walk as far as the Kodama pond and back, as
the torii gates thin out further up the trail.

Fushimi-Inari is located next to JR Inari station
(you can make use of your JR Pass again at
last!), only five minutes from Kyoto station on the
Nara line by local train. If time allows, check out
neighbouring **Tofukuji** Temple just one stop
along (or within walking distance from Fushimi
Inari), a Zen temple which looks particularly
spectacular when the autumn colours are on
show.

Insider tip:

- Be on the lookout for one of Japan's most
unusual snacks, *Suzume-yaki* (barbecued
sparrows on sticks) which are sold in some of
the small shops lining the winding road which
leads back down towards the station. These
small birds are cooked and eaten whole, and
have a somewhat earthy flavour. A unique

delicacy, many Japanese people have never even tried them!

**Arashiyama **

Nestled on the western edges of Kyoto, Arashiyama is a picturesque district with enough to see and do to occupy a full day, although an afternoon should suffice. The **Togetsukyo Bridge** is Arashiyama's unmistakable main landmark, spanning the wide and slow-flowing Katsura River, while nearby shops and cafes serve up assortments of Japanese sweets and *machya* (green tea) ice cream. Just north of the river, **Tenryuji Temple** (500 yen) is a world heritage site with attractive gardens, and slightly further north again are the famous **bamboo groves** which have an eerie sense of tranquillity, especially at dawn or dusk.
Just south of the river is the **Iwatayama Monkey Park** (550 yen), which involves a ten minute hike up the mountain to a hilltop clearing where large groups of monkeys roam freely and can be fed. There are also great views of Kyoto from the park.

Arashiyama can be reached from Kyoto station by taking the train to JR Saga-Arashiyama station (15 minutes). Alternatively, from Kawaramachi you can take the Hankyu line (changing at Katsura) to Hankyu Arashiyama station (20 minutes, 220 yen), or use the Keifuku

Railway from Omiya station in central Kyoto (20 minutes, 210 yen).
There are also many buses from central Kyoto. The #28 Kyoto City bus leaves from Kyoto station and takes about half an hour.

Insider tip:

- On the south side of the river from the bridge, walk past the entrance to the Monkey Park and continue following the path as it follows the river. After about 15 minutes you should arrive at a scenic and rocky area where you can get close to the water and wave at the boats as they pass by.
For the even more adventurous, the path continues upstream along a narrow and wild trail (watch out for the giant hornets!) before reaching an area of rapids, rocks and plunge pools which some thrill seekers use for cooling down in the summer (enter at your own risk).

Ryoan-ji

Tucked away in a quiet corner of northwest Kyoto, **Ryoan-ji Temple** is home to Japan's most famous rock garden. The origins and the meaning of the garden's layout are unknown, but there are 15 rocks carefully laid out, and from whatever vantage point you take, one of them always remains hidden from view.

(◉ www.ryoanji.jp/smph/eng ☼8am-5pm, ¥500, 616-8001)

Ryoan-ji can be reached by bus from Kyoto station (30 minutes, 230 yen) or by taking the Keifuku Kitano line to Ryoan-ji Michi station, from where it is a ten minute walk.
It is also only a twenty minute walk from the Golden Pavilion.

Nijo Castle

A UNESCO world heritage site, Nijo Castle dates back to 1603 and was the Kyoto residence of the first *shogun* of the Edo period, Tokugawa Ieyasu. The castle is made up of three main areas; the Honmaru (main defence, including the palace buildings), the Ninomaru (secondary circle of defence) and the gardens (with their surrounding stone walls and moat). It has been said that the palace buildings are the best surviving example of such elite architecture from Japan's feudal era, and they feature the famous nightingale floors which squeak when stepped on, to alert the occupants of intruders.

Entry is 600 yen, with good English audio guides available for 500 yen. The castle gardens are particularly scenic during cherry blossom season and in late November when the autumn colours are at their best.

(◉ www2.city.kyoto.lg.jp/bunshi/nijojo/english ☼ 8.45am-5pm, ¥600, 604-8301)

Nijo Castle is fairly centrally located and is just a short walk from Nijo-Mae station on the Tozai subway line. Also served by buses 9,50,101 from Kyoto station (15 minutes, 230 yen) or bus number 12 from Shijo-Kawaramachi (15 minutes, 230 yen).

Imperial Palace Gardens

Until the capital moved to Tokyo in 1868, this was the official residence of Japan's Imperial family, and although the palace can't be entered, it is possible to freely explore the grounds. There are also free tours (including English) of some of the palace buildings (and nearby off-site villas), and whereas in previous years an advanced reservation was necessary to participate, since the summer of 2016 the procedure has been much simplified. A limited number of tickets become available from 11am on the day of the tour at the palace or villa in question, with tour spaces filled up on a first-come-first-served basis.
It is probably only worth getting a tour ticket for visitors particularly interested in the history of the Imperial Palace and the Imperial family, as most people will probably be content with just a leisurely stroll around the main gardens.

(◙ www.kunaicho.go.jp/e-event/kyototsunen-
sankan-sks.html ☼ 9am-4pm or 5pm depending
on season, closed Mondays, ¥free, 602-0881)

Kyoto Imperial Park itself is free to enter and is a
pleasant escape from the hustle and bustle of
the city, but can seem a bit underwhelming
compared to some of the other attractions in
Kyoto.

To reach the park, take the Karasuma subway
line from Kyoto station to either Marutamachi or
Imadegawa stations (10 minutes).

8. Must-do daytrips near Kyoto

Kyoto is probably the most well-known city in Kansai, a region of historical and cultural importance, and the area has enough to see and do to fill a full trip itinerary on its own. With Kansai International airport (built on its own manmade island just south of Osaka) serving the area, visiting has never been easier.

Kansai (which means 'west of the barrier', an allusion to the former checkpoints which separated the region from Kanto to the east) is both compact in size but incredibly varied, from the imposing sprawl of Osaka, a Japanese metropolis with a friendly side, to cosmopolitan Kobe wedged between the mountains and the sea, to rural Nara with its unmissable world heritage sites.

Most visitors set their focus on Kyoto when it comes to the Kansai area, but it is well worth exploring the region a little further. If pushed for time, then a day exploring Osaka, the region's biggest city and culinary hotspot, should be just enough time to get a feel for the place. This can then be followed by a day in Nara, a charming and historical city, and small enough to be mostly explored on foot. In fact, Osaka makes a great base from which to explore the region (even if Kyoto is your main sightseeing priority), with an abundance of hotels and numerous (and quick) transport links to the surrounding cities.

Osaka **

This large merchant and port city (population of around 3 million) has a reputation for good food and friendly locals. Until fairly recently it wasn't really on the tourist map, but nearby **Universal Studios Japan** (◉ www.usj.co.jp/e) is a big draw now. Osaka is not a city full of tourist attractions, but it is a place that rewards those who take time to explore its streets and absorb the atmosphere. Check out (◉ www.osaka-info.jp/en) to find out what's going on in the city.

Osaka is generally divided into the *Kita* (north) and *Minami* (south) areas. *Kita* is the business and shopping district, focused around fashionable Umeda, while Namba and Shinsaibashi in *Minami* are better known for their nightlife and entertainment (as well as shopping). Numerous subway lines connect all parts of the city, and for those with a JR Pass, the JR loop line has stops close to most of the main attractions. A full day in Osaka should be enough to see the main sights.

Probably Osaka's most famous landmark, **Osaka Castle **** and the surrounding park grounds are a must. The castle was originally built in the late 16th century, and was subsequently destroyed and rebuilt a number of times. The current main castle tower was rebuilt as recently as 1997, and while the views from the top are interesting, the inside is disappointingly modern (and even has an elevator!) so it's not vital to pay the 600 yen to enter. Enjoy the impressive original stone ramparts and views from around the castle grounds instead.

There is good access from all directions, but the most convenient station is Osakajokoen on the JR loop line.

In the northwest of the city, the **Umeda Sky Building** ** is just a ten minute walk from Osaka station and despite not being the tallest building in Osaka it boasts some of the city's best views from its 39th floor open air 'floating garden observatory'. Price of admission is 1000 yen, with last entry at 22:00, and the night-time views of the city are fantastic. Also check out the basement level for restaurants along a recreation of a Showa era street.

In the south of the city, the **Dotonbori** ** and **Shinsaibashi** areas (close to Namba and Shinsaibashi stations) are the main shopping and entertainment districts, the former most famous for its neon lights and countless eating options, Shinsaibashi being the place for brand shopping heaven. From the *Dotonbori* bridge you can spot local landmarks such as the Glico Running Man and the *Kani Doraku* (moving crab) signs, and the covered shopping arcade (*shoutengai*) is reputed to be the longest of its kind in Japan.

Nearby **Den Den Town** (close to Nipponbashi, Namba and Ebisu-cho subway stations) is famous for its electronics stores, and has become a mecca for anime, cosplay and videogame fans. The area also has a number of maid cafes, where cute girls in maid costumes serve you tea at slightly inflated prices.
Just west of Shinsaibashi is **Ame-mura**, or America Town, a cool and young area centred around Triangle Park; it is full of quirky clothes shops, foreign-style bars and restaurants and interesting fashion choices.

For a taste of old Osaka, head to **Shinsekai **** (just north of JR Shin-Imamiya station on the loop line), an area of slightly dingy streets and countless *kushikatsu* restaurants surrounding the local landmark, Tsutenkaku Tower. Shinsekai actually means 'New World', but the district has a very dated and gritty feel to it now, as nothing has really changed since the early 20th century. It's interesting to wander around in the early evening however, and the *kushikatsu* (fried items on sticks) are an Osaka speciality. Just to the east of Shinsekai is Tennoji Zoo, which has quite impressive reptile and nocturnal houses, but the rest of it is quite small and overly concrete, and some of the animals are in a bit of a sorry state.

Directly south of Tsutenkaku Tower you can find **Spa World**, a multi-floor, multi-bath (European and Asian themed) hot spring and swimming pool complex (entry from 1200 yen).

Getting there: Kansai International airport is about an hour from Osaka by train or bus (see the previous chapter), and if coming from Tokyo, the *shinkansen* stops at Shin-Osaka, which has JR and subway connections to the rest of the city.
From Kyoto station, there are many local and rapid JR trains to Osaka station (Special Rapid Service trains take 28 minutes), and the *shinkansen* to Shin-Osaka takes less than 15 minutes!

Insider tips:

- If you are going to be spending a bit of time in Osaka, it is worthwhile investing in the **Osaka Pass** (◙ www.osaka-info.jp/osp/en/index.html). Valid for either 1 or 2 days, it gives you unlimited travel on the subways, buses and private railway lines (not JR, but you can use your JR pass for that), as well as offering free entry or discounts to a number of attractions.

- Explore one of Osaka's most popular areas for food and drink (but not full of tourists) by taking the loop line to JR **Kyobashi** station and heading right (east) after exiting the north ticket gates; you'll discover a rabbit warren of standing bars, gritty izakayas, and a taste of the real Osaka. Or instead head left (west) out of the ticket gates for plusher restaurants and drinking establishments.

- Catch a baseball game. Even if you don't know the rules, an evening watching Japanese pro baseball is an entertaining experience, with the fans sometimes being more lively than the action on the field! Hanshin Tigers are the big local team, but tickets tend to sell out quickly, so instead head to the Kyocera Dome to watch the **Orix Buffaloes** play under an impressive space age roof. It's usually possible to buy tickets on the door (prices start from around 2000 yen) and the season runs from late March to October. (◙ www.buffaloes.co.jp/english ¥2000)

Nara *

As the first permanent capital of Japan in 710, Nara is a city of historical and political significance which defies its small and compact size. Even if you are all *temple-ed* out by Kyoto, a visit to Nara is still highly recommended as it is pleasant and green, packed full of world heritage sites, and virtually everything of note can be seen on foot. In fact, Nara probably makes for one of the best day trips in the Kansai area and should be included on your itinerary if at all possible.

See (◉ www.narashikanko.or.jp/en) for an introduction to Nara's history and cultural significance.

From JR Nara station, leave the east exit and look for the 'Super Hotel' JR Nara Ekimae near the crossroads. The narrow street next to this is called *Sanjo Dori*, and it's a fifteen minute walk up this bustling street towards **Kofukuji Temple** and its five-story pagoda (the second tallest in Japan). The grounds are free to walk around and are full of interesting buildings, as well as the National Treasure Museum which houses a fine collection of Buddhist art (600 yen).

Just a few minutes walk from here is **Nara Park** ** which is home to the National Museum, and more famously, about one thousand sacred (and disconcertingly tame) deer. They roam around freely, but can be coaxed into bowing if offered special crackers available from vendors.

Not far north from the museum is **Isuien Garden**, one of Nara's most beautiful and classically-styled gardens. Entry is 900 yen, but it a peaceful escape from the nearby crowds. Those on a budget can visit the **Yoshiki-en** garden next door which is somewhat smaller, but foreigners can enter for free if they show their passport.

The northern end of the park is home to Nara's most famous landmark, the impressive **Todaiji**

Temple **, which is not only the world's largest wooden building but also houses one of the largest bronze statues of Buddha in the country. It is a genuinely impressive sight, and if you could only visit one temple during the whole of your stay in Japan, then this would be a great choice. The approach via **Nandai-mon Gate** (with its ominous looking gatekeepers) is the best way to get there. Watch out for all the deer and selfie sticks though.
(◉ www.todaiji.or.jp/english ☼ 8am-4.30pm winter/7.30am-5.30pm summer, ¥500, 630-8211)

To the east of Todaiji is **Nigatsu-do Temple**, a collection of temple buildings located slightly off the main tourist trail and so a good place for meditation and reflection. There are also great views out over Nara from the large veranda of the main temple building.

These sites can all easily be visited in an afternoon trip from Kyoto or Osaka, but if you have more time in Nara then **Kasuga Taisha** in the eastern part of Nara Park is a beautiful shrine with extensive grounds (free to enter, apart from the inner sanctuary, 500 yen), all of which are lit up by hundreds of lanterns during the Lantern Festivals of February and August. The surrounding area is known as **Kazugayama Genshirin** and it is one of Nara's hidden secrets; a quiet wooded hideaway, with a plethora of short trails which weave through the pristine primeval forest. The crowds really thin out the further away you get from Kasuga Taisha, and the mixture of nature and mysterious old shrines hidden away in the trees makes for quite a mystical experience, especially at dawn or dusk (be careful not to get lost!).

Back towards the city and southeast of the station, the **Naramachi** area is an old merchant's district where traditional townhouses and old storehouses have been preserved, with a few now functioning as rustic teahouses, cafes and boutiques.

Getting there: Nara is very easy to visit as a daytrip or half-daytrip from either Kyoto (44 minutes) or Osaka (JR Namba or JR Osaka, both 50 minutes). The Kintetsu railway also has links from both cities, with trains terminating at Kintetsu Nara station, which is just a short walk west of Nara Park.

Insider tips:

- For some traditional Nara cuisine, head to **Hiraso** (not far from Naramachi) and try the *kakinoha* sushi (smoked mackerel or salmon wrapped in persimmon leaves), a Nara speciality. They serve other dishes too and have an English menu.
(◉ www.hiraso.jp/lang/english.html ☼10am-8.30pm/closed Mondays, 630-8374)

- Somewhat south of the city itself (30 minutes on the JR Sakurai line, Miwa station) is **Omiwa Shrine**, the oldest Shinto shrine in Japan, and a place of great cultural significance and peaceful beauty. The shrine is not dedicated to any particular god, but rather to the mountain which it sits at the foot of. For a pleasant escape into the Japanese countryside, this is a great choice. (☼ 24hrs a day, ¥free, 633-0001)

Kobe

This attractive and (by Japanese standards) cosmopolitan city sandwiched between the Inland Sea and the Rokko mountains is most famous for the succulent high-grade beef that bears the city's name, but it also makes for an enjoyable half-daytrip from Osaka or Kyoto.

In 1995 Kobe was struck by the Great Hanshin Awaji Earthquake, which killed over 5000 people and destroyed tens of thousands of buildings. The city has been completely rebuilt now, but it is possible to get a sense of the scale of the disaster by visiting the **Earthquake Memorial Museum** (600 yen, closed most Mondays), a fifteen minute walk from Nada station on the JR Kobe line.

Sannomiya and **Motomachi** are the city's main shopping and commercial districts, the latter of which is home to one of the biggest Chinatown's in Japan. Further west, just outside Kobe JR station is **Kobe Harborland**, a popular dating spot with waterside cafes, restaurants and amusements.

Further west again at **Suma** (JR Suma station) there is a beach popular with a younger crowd in the summer; it's far from being Japan's most beautiful beach, but the cool waters can be a welcome respite from the oppressive summer heat and the beachside food shacks are great for people watching.

The **Shin-Kobe Ropeway** whisks visitors up the southern side of the Rokko mountain range, and the observation deck at the top offers great views of the city and Osaka bay, especially at night. There is also a large aromatic herb garden, as well as a café and a restaurant. It's possible to follow an easy hiking trail back down to the station, passing by Nunobiki Waterfall on the way (takes less than an hour in total). A return ropeway ticket including entrance to the herb garden is 1400 yen, and the ropeway station is five minutes walk west of Shin-Kobe station.

For those looking to escape the city on a slightly more strenuous hike, try the **Rokku Gaaden** course, which can be reached from JR Ashiya station (and a few other stations), and snakes its way up the mountainside over numerous rocky outcrops which are great fun to climb. Look out for wild boar too, as they are frequently spotted in the area (don't feed them as they can be a little aggressive). Allow about 3 hours return. See (◉ www.japanhike.wordpress.com) for full hike details.

Getting there: Sannomiya is Kobe's main station, easily reached from Osaka on the JR Special Rapid Service in just 21 minutes. From Kyoto the same service takes about 51 minutes. Shin-Kobe is the *shinkansen* station if you want to travel there even faster.

Insider tip:

- Kobe beef is what put the city on the map, but finding somewhere to sample this high-grade *wagyu* is not always as easy as you'd expect. Prices can vary wildly, and dinner prices are never cheap, so for those on a budget, lookout for lunchtime sets which can sometimes start as low as 3000 yen per person.

Wakkoqu offers a variety of courses to suit all budgets, and the beef is of the highest quality. (◉ www.wakkoqu.com/english/food.html ☼12pm-10pm, ¥3500-15000, 650-0002)

Steak Land Kobe has a convenient location and is at the more affordable end of the spectrum. (☼11am-10pm, ¥2000-4000, 650-0012)

Tor Road Steak Aoyama is a family run restaurant near Sannomiya which lives up to its great reviews.
(◉ www.steakaoyama.com ☼12pm-9pm, closed Wednesdays, ¥2000-6000, 650-0011)

Kobe Beef Yazawa West and **Kisshokichi** are establishments in a chain of high quality beef restaurants scattered across the city.
(◉ www.koubegyuu.com/en/shop/yazawa-west ☼11am-10pm, ¥3000-7000, 650-0022)

Most high-end hotels also have a *teppanyaki* grill serving *wagyu*, so it is always worth checking their menus too.

Koya-san

Recently becoming very popular with overseas visitors, Koyasan is the name given to the sacred mountains where a small temple town belonging to the Shingon Buddhism sect developed from 826. Kobo Daishi was one of the sect's most important figures, and he searched for years for the perfect place to build the religion's founding temple, which he eventually found in the high wooded peaks close to the border of Osaka and Wakayama prefectures. Since that time, over one hundred temples were built, the main one being **Kongobuji**, which is the head temple of Shingon Buddhism. For 500 yen visitors can enter this impressive temple and tour the many rooms, with the chance of tea and sweets in the large tatami hall, and the rock garden behind the temple is the largest of its kind in Japan.

Okunoin is another temple which is also the site of Kobo Daishi's mausoleum, and the path there winds its way through a rich forest full of gravestones and tombs, in what is the largest cemetery in Japan. A visit at dawn or dusk can be an atmospheric experience indeed.

Undoubtedly the best way to really sample the magic of Koyasan is to stay at one of the temples which offer overnight stays. **Temple lodgings** are known as *shukubo* and guests can experience the simple life of Buddhist monks, sleeping on futons, enjoying wonderful vegetarian food and there is usually the chance to wake up early to participate in the morning prayers.

Prices start at around 9000 yen per night (including dinner, breakfast and hot baths) and can be booked online at (◙ eng.shukubo.net), or through Japanese Guest Houses (◙ www.japaneseguesthouses.com) or Japanican (◙ www.japanican.com/en).

Getting there: Take the Nankai Railway from Osaka's Namba or Shin-Imamiya stations (not covered by the JR Pass) on the Nankai Koya Line to Gokurakubashi station (limited express is 80 minutes and 1650 yen, an express or rapid express train takes 100 mins for 870 yen). From there, transfer to the cablecar (5 minutes, 390 yen) to the top of the mountain, and then take a ten minute bus ride to Senjuinbashi bus stop (290 yen).

Insider tip:

- There are a number of discount tickets to save a bit of money. The Koyasan World Heritage Ticket (2860 yen) combines travel from Osaka to Koyasan, entry to all the attractions and use of the buses around town. It can be bought from Osaka's Nankai stations.
The Combination Ticket (2000 yen) provides entry to all of Koyasan's main sights, is valid for two days, and can be bought from the tourist office or any of the main points of interest.
A 1-Day Bus Pass (830 yen) lets you ride any of Koyasan's buses freely for one day, and can be purchased from the upper station of the cablecar.

Himeji

A small and pleasant city less than one hour from Osaka, the main reason to visit is for the newly refurbished **Himeji Castle**, a world heritage site and national treasure. Over 400 years old and known as the 'white heron castle', this is probably the most spectacular castle in Japan, and makes for a good half-day trip.
(◉ www.himejicastle.jp/en ☼ 9am-5pm, ¥1000, 670-0012)

Getting there: The JR Special Rapid Service from Osaka takes about 60 minutes, while the *shinkansen* from Shin-Osaka is a speedy 30 minutes.

Hiroshima

Hiroshima is not particularly close to Kyoto, and is not even in Kansai (it's the main city of the Chugoku region), but with an early start it is possible to visit the city as a daytrip from either Kyoto or Osaka. Hiroshima became infamous as the first city in the world to be targeted by a nuclear weapon, when on August 6th, 1945 the American Air Force dropped a 15 kiloton nuclear bomb on the city, destroying everything within a 2km radius and killing an estimated 80,000 people. The **Peace Memorial Park** and **A-Bomb Dome** are stark reminders of the horrors of the event, and no visitor can help but be moved during a visit. Admission to the museum is 200 yen, and it can be accessed by taking tram line 2 or 6 to Genpaku-Domu Mae from Hiroshima station.

If you have more time in Hiroshima then it is well worth taking the 10 minute JR ferry (free with a JR Pass, 260 yen otherwise) out to **Miyajima** island. From JR Miyajimaguchi station it is a short walk to the ferry pier. The island is home to Itsukushima Shrine, famous for its big red torii gate which seems to float on the water, and is one of Japan's three most famous views. Deer roam the island, and you can see wild monkeys if you take the cable car up to the top of Mt. Misen (1800 yen return). It is worth spending the night in a traditional *ryokan* on the island, but if time is tight then you can visit the shrine and see the deer all within an hour.

See (◙ www.visithiroshima.net) for more details of everything.

Getting there: Hiroshima can be reached in about 100 minutes from Shin-Osaka station by *shinkansen* (remember, the JR Pass is not valid for the fastest Nozomi trains). From Kyoto it takes about 120 minutes.

9. If you have more time....

In the previous chapters we discovered the places you simply must visit to say you've 'done' Japan; the capital city Tokyo, the iconic Mt. Fuji, and the historic Kansai area. But what if you have more time? If you have a JR rail pass (and it really is recommended), then your options greatly increase, as there are interesting places to visit all over the country.
The following destinations are all good options to consider in addition to the main itinerary, or to form the basis of further trips to the country in the future.

Central Japan

The *Chubu* region is a large and varied area covering a vast swathe of central Honshu west of Tokyo and east of Kansai. There are many interesting places to visit, especially for those looking to escape the big cities, and with its good transport links from both Tokyo and Kyoto/Osaka, exploration of the region is relatively simple. As well as Mt. Fuji, some of the biggest mountains in Japan are to be found here, especially in the northern, central and southern Japan Alps, and they attract outdoor lovers from all over the country.

Takayama

A small and pleasant historic city nestling deep in the heart of Gifu prefecture, Takayama has seen a tourist boom in recent years, so much so in fact, that JR Takayama station was completely redeveloped in 2016 to cope with the influx of visitors. Also sometimes referred to as Hida-Takayama (in reference to the old Hida Province) the city has long been a local centre of importance, and due to its relative isolation and altitude, and the city still retains much of its old charm and uniqueness. Takayama makes for a good base from which to explore this rural part of Japan, as there is good access to the nearby Japan Alps, numerous winter ski resorts and the famous thatched houses of Shirakawa-go. See (◙ www.hida.jp/english) for lots of useful tourist information about the city and other places in the region.

Most of Takayama's main attractions can be found by taking the east exit from Takayama station and walking directly east for about 10 minutes. This is where you will find the picturesque **Old Town**, where whole streets of Edo-period merchant houses remain intact and a walk around the area really does feel like stepping back in time. The southern part of the Old Town, centred around Sannomachi Street, has many old houses, shops, museums and sake breweries (for which the city is famous). This is also close to **Shiroyama Park**, where visitors can see the old castle ruins and follow the easy but interesting Higashiyama walking course (ask for a map at the tourist information office outside JR Takayama station) which loops back into town via a district of historic temples. **Hida no Sato** (Hida Folk Village) is an impressive open-air museum where over 30 historic buildings from around the Hida region were relocated to create a fascinating time capsule of an attraction. A wide range of buildings are preserved there, including some of the famous thatched farm buildings from nearby Shirakawa-go, and visitors are free to enter and explore all of them. Every morning the fireplaces are lit too, to recreate the feeling of a lived-in Edo village, with all of its authentic sights and smells. The Folk Village costs 700 yen to enter and is a 30 minute walk west of Takayama station, or a 10 minute bus ride on the 'Sarubobo bus' (210 yen, or 620 yen for a one-day pass). There is also a discount ticket combining the round trip bus ticket with entrance to the village for 930 yen (ask at the bus centre).

Possibly the biggest draw to Takayama is the famous **Takayama Festival**, which takes place twice a year, in the spring (April 14-15) and again in the autumn (October 9-10). Each festival features a wide range of processions, performances and ornately decorated floats being carried through the streets, both during the day and in the early evening. Widely regarded as one of Japan's most beautiful festivals, people come from far and wide and hotels are often booked up months in advance, so plan ahead accordingly.

Getting there: From Tokyo, take the *shinkansen* to Nagoya (100 or 120 minutes) and then change to a JR Hida limited express train for Takayama (140 minutes). The whole journey is covered by the JR Pass (if using a Hikari bullet train to Nagoya).
There are also highway buses run by Keio (◉ highway-buses.jp/takayama)
and Nohi (◉ www.nouhibus.co.jp/english) which take about 5.5 hours for 6,690 yen.
From Kyoto and Osaka there is a direct train called the JR limited express Wide View Hida (once a day, leaves Osaka at 7.58am, covered by the JR Pass). It's also possible to take the *shinkansen* to Nagoya and go on from there.
There are also frequent buses from Matsumoto city.

Shirakawa-go and Gokayama

These are two small regions deep in the mountainous Japanese countryside, where old-fashioned villages and farmhouses have not only been preserved, but remain very much lived-in. Both areas were designated together as one UNESCO World Heritage site, but they actually incorporate a number of small villages which are famous for the gassho-zukuri farmhouses, with their steep thatched roofs, built to withstand heavy snowfall and the inside spaces of which are used to cultivate silkworms.

The villages are very photogenic in any season, but particularly in winter, when deep snow blankets the region and some of the buildings are attractively lit-up. **Ogimachi** is the largest village in Shirakawa-go and is a popular day trip from Takayama. To really experience the traditional ambience of the place, it is possible to stay the night in one of the farmhouses, many of which now serve as *minshuku* (family-run B&B's). The villages of Gokayama are slightly less convenient to access, requiring a bus change at Ogimachi, but for this reason they tend to be less crowded and feel even more rustic. The largest village is **Ainokura**, which has a number of *minshuku*, museums and traditional private houses. **Suganuma** village is smaller, but has the same kind of attractions and is easy to explore on foot.

Getting there: Takayama is a good base from which to visit, and there are regular buses taking about 60 minutes from there.
(◉ www.nouhibus.co.jp/english, ¥2470).

If coming directly from Tokyo, take the Hokuriku *shinkansen* to Toyama (130-170 minutes, 12,500 yen) and then change to a bus for Shirakawa-go (90 minutes, 1700 yen).
It is also possible to take the *shinkansen* to Kanazawa and take a bus from there. Or from

Shin-Takaoka station, buses bound for
Shirakawa-go also stop at Gokayama on the
way.
(◉ www.gokayama-
info.jp/en/img/access/english.pdf)

Matsumoto

Home to one of Japan's most beautiful (and
mostly intact) castles, Matsumoto is a small city
steeped in history and is a popular gateway for
exploring the backcountry of Japan, with its
convenient connections to Kamikochi and the
Japan Alps.

The main tourist attraction is undoubtedly
Matsumoto Castle. It has a somewhat unique
structure and layout amongst castles in Japan,
and its contrasting black and white colour
scheme gives it a memorable look too. The
castle dates back to the late 16th century, and
much of the wooden interior, complete with
secret openings for defence and steep wooden
stairs remain in place. This makes it one of the
best preserved and most interesting castles to
visit in the whole of the country. To get there it is
just a 15 minute walk north east of Matsumoto
station, and entry is 610 yen.

Just south of the castle and close to the city
centre is the **Nakamachi** district, an area of
nicely preserved white merchants buildings,
some of which now serve as shops and *ryokans*.

Insider tip:

- Try some of the local Matsumoto delicacies. Zaru-soba (buckwheat noodles, served cold with a range of toppings) is probably the most well-known one, and **Metoba Soba** is the place to eat them.
(◙ www.metobasoba.com (*Japanese*) ☼ 11am-7pm/closed Wednesdays and the 3rd Tuesday every month, ¥700-2000, 390-0811)

- Much less well-known, and not for the squeamish are *inago* (fried crickets) and *hachinoko* (bee larvae), both of which used to form part of the diet for rural communities in the region. Some *izakayas* will have them on the menu.

Getting there: Matsumoto is easily reached from Tokyo's JR Shinjuku station on an Azusa or Super Azusa limited express train (2.5 hours, 6000-7000 yen).
Highway buses are another cheaper option. They leave hourly from Shinjuku bus terminal to Matsumoto (about 3 hours, 3500 yen). A roundtrip ticket can be had for 6100 yen.

Kamikochi and the Japan Alps

The Japan Alps is the name given to a number of huge mountain ranges which stretch all the way across central Honshu, from the Sea of

Japan coast in the north right down to the Pacific coast. There are three main regions, known as the *Kita* (North), *Chuo* (Central) and *Minami* (South) Alps, and all are home to many mountains over 3000m in height and spectacular alpine scenery. Many of the mountains remain snow- capped from about late November to early June, so hiking is usually restricted to the summer and autumn seasons (unless you are an expert).

For good English information on hiking in the Japan Alps, and other hikes around the country, check out (◉ www.japanhike.wordpress.com).

Kamikochi is a small and secluded alpine resort deep in the heart of the *Kita* Alps (North Alps) from where some of the best long hikes in Japan begin, but many people also visit for a daytrip, and this is easily done from Takayama or Matsumoto. The **Kappabashi bridge** is a popular spot from which to take photos of the impressive Hotaka mountains, and there are a number of easy walks from there to enjoy the scenery and perhaps spot a Japanese macaque in the wild (they are very common on the paths around Kamikochi).

Myojin Pond has beautiful reflections of the nearby mountains and is an easy and pleasant stroll along flat woodland paths. Allow 2 hours for the full loop. Likewise, **Taisho Pond** is famous for wonderful reflections if the weather is good, and is also a two hour walk along easy paths. The forests and rivers on both of these walks are some of the most pristine you will ever see.

There are also a number of places to stay in Kamikochi, along with a few shops and restaurants and even some hot baths. Kamikochi can be very busy on summer weekends, national holidays and in the early fall for the autumn colours, so if possible try to visit on a weekday to avoid the crowds. Also be aware that the bus to Kamikochi (no cars are allowed) only runs from Golden Week (late April) until mid-November, as the resort shuts down for winter.

Getting there: Kamikochi is easily accessed by bus from Takayama and Matsumoto. From Takayama, take a bus to Hirayu Onsen (one hour, 1570 yen), and then change there for a bus to Kamikochi (25 minutes, 1160 yen).
From Matsumoto station, take the Matsumoto Electric Railway to Shin-Shimashima station (30 minutes), and then change to a bus bound for Kamikochi (one hour, 2450 yen). The JR Pass is not valid for this train or bus.
There are also some direct express buses to Kamikochi from Tokyo and Kyoto/Osaka (◙ www.alpico.co.jp/access/english).

Be careful not to miss the last bus out of Kamikochi, it usually leaves at about 5pm, so be sure to check at the bus terminal before going off to explore the area.

Tateyama Kurobe Alpine Route

Deep in the mountains of Toyama is the **Tateyama Kurobe Alpine Route**, the first section of which has a bus route winding through a spectacular snow corridor with snow walls almost 20m high (April to June). A full traverse of the route takes you right through the heart of the North Alps and out the other side, using buses, ropeways and cable cars, and is popular throughout the summer and early autumn. See (◙ www.alpen-route.com/en) for information.

Kanazawa

The three prefectures of Fukui, Ishikawa and Toyama make up the Hokuriku area on the Sea of Japan coast. The main draw for tourists here is the attractive traditional city of **Kanazawa** (recently made accessible by *shinkansen* from Tokyo), which is almost like a smaller, and possibly even prettier version of Kyoto. During the Edo period, Kanazawa was an important trade and cultural hub, and was the second biggest city (after Kyoto) to escape bombing during World War II, and so many of its historical assets remain intact. Renowned for its great seafood and various places of interest, the city has become a popular weekend getaway for Tokyoites and Kansai residents alike.

Kanazawa's number one attraction is undoubtedly **Kenrokuen**, one of 'Japan's three most beautiful landscape gardens' and a must-visit.

Check (◙ www.pref.ishikawa.jp/siro-niwa/kenrokuen/e) for details. Entry is only 310 yen, or free if you arrive very early in the morning (time changes depending on season, but we're talking 5am early!).

There are a number of buses from Kanazawa station which make stops at the garden, including the JR bus (free for JR Pass holders). The popular **Kanazawa Loop Bus** covers most of the tourist areas including the garden too. (◙ www.kanazawa-tourism.com/eng/guide/guide3.php ☼ every 15 minutes, ¥200)

Another popular attraction is **Ninjadera**, or Myoryuji Temple as it is actually called (◙ www.myouryuji.or.jp/en.html). The temple was built by the Maeda clan in the Edo period, and while it has nothing directly to do with ninja, it earned its nickname thanks to the many secretive defences found all over the building, including secret corridors, escape routes, hidden rooms and traps. Entry is 1000 yen, and although the guided tours are in Japanese, some good English books explain all the details. Take the left loop of the Kanazawa Loop Bus (15 minutes, 200 yen) to Hirokoji bus stop, from where it is a five minute walk.

For more history, visit **Nagamachi**, the former samurai district, or any of the three *chaya* (teahouse) districts, namely Higashi Chayagai, Nishi Chayagai and Kazuemachi. All three have quaint traditional streets, preserved old-style houses and numerous shops and tearooms. **Higashi Chayagai** is probably the biggest and most interesting of the three, and can be reached by taking the right loop of the Loop Bus for 10 minutes and getting off at Hashibacho. **Kanazawa Castle** is located centrally, and despite being burned down and destroyed multiple times, it is now in the long and slow process of reconstruction, and the main buildings are complete and open for visitors. The castle park is a nice place to stroll around, especially during cherry blossom season.

For something a little more modern, a visit to the **21st Century Museum of Contemporary Art** is well worth considering. Located just next door to Kenrokuen, it only opened in 2004 but has already become of the most popular art galleries in the country, housing a range of works by artists from all over the world. The building itself is circular in form, with no obvious front, back or even main entrance, so that visitors approach the building (and the art within) from not just the one, same direction. Leandro Erlich's 'Swimming Pool' (where people appear to be under the water) is one of the museum's most famous works and a favourite for art-loving Instagramers. The museum can be accessed by any of the aforementioned buses from Kanazawa station, get off at Hirosaka bus stop (10 minutes, 200 yen). Each exhibition has a different fee, entry is generally around 1000 yen.

Getting there: From Tokyo, take the Hokuriku *shinkansen* to Kanazawa station (3 hours, 14,000 yen), which is covered by the JR Pass. From Osaka and Kyoto there are limited express Thunderbird trains (160 minutes, 7400 yen) running twice an hour, and they are also covered by the JR Pass.
Kanazawa can also be easily reached from Takayama by bus or train.

Hokkaido

Located in the far north of the country, Hokkaido is Japan's second largest island and its biggest wilderness area. Winters are long and cold with heaps of snow, but during the summer the landscape of green, open pastures dotted with rural farmsteads means there is almost a European feel to it.

The centre of Hokkaido is dominated by the **Daisetsuzan National Park**, a huge area of remote mountains, volcanic landscapes and inviting hot springs. The park is littered with hiking trails, the longest of which can take the best part of a week to complete, and there are always lingering snowfields, even in the height of summer, so hikers must be suitably prepared. There are however a number of easier walks, the best of which starts from **Asahidake Onsen,** a popular hot spring resort deep in the mountains, from where it is possible to ride the ropeway up to 1600m to see the impressive alpine landscape, steaming sulphur vents, pockets of remaining snow and countless wildflowers (in the summer). There are a number of small loop walks suitable for families, or a more arduous 4 hour return hike to the top of Asahi-dake (2290m), Hokkaido's highest point.

The even more remote **Shiretoko** peninsular in eastern Hokkaido is virtually untouched by humans and is home to the largest population of brown bears in the country. Boat trips along the coast are a good way to try to spot some of these elusive creatures from a safe distance (◙ www.kamuiwakka.jp/english-booking.php). Also in the east is **Akan National Park**, a region of beautiful pristine lakes, active volcanoes and simmering hot springs.

Back in central Hokkaido, the pretty towns of **Furano** and **Biei** are well-known for their surrounding European-esque hilly patchwork landscapes, with the end of July/early August the best time to visit the extensive and fragrant lavender fields and flower meadows. It's also a good time to sample the wide range of local produce, and seasonal specialities such as lavender ice-cream.

Sapporo is an attractive city and the largest urban area in Hokkaido, with a modern grid-based layout, and attractions including the Sapporo Beer Museum and the winter Snow Festival. It also serves as the main gateway to Hokkaido, with rail and bus connections to many corners of the island, and with regular domestic and international flights from nearby New Chitose Airport.

Also not far from Sapporo, **Niseko** has great powder snow and some of the best skiing in this part of the world. Recently popular with foreigners (particularly Australians), the resort villages in the area have a very western feel and are usually packed in the winter (so best to book accommodation well in advance), but summer is the off-season and is also a pleasant (and quiet) time to visit, with good hiking nearby (Yotei-zan is an inactive volcano often likened to Mt. Fuji due to its shape, although only half the height).

The far north of Hokkaido is extremely rural and remote, but the port of **Wakkanai** is the northernmost city in Japan and has a unique frontier flavour of its own (spot the Russian script on road signs) and a plethora of great seafood. There are regular ferries to the nearby islands of **Rishiri** and **Rebun** (2 hours one way), the former of which is an extinct volcano jutting out of the sea to a height of 1721 metres, and offers good hiking, camping and world-class *uni* (sea urchin). Rebun is a smaller and more gently formed island, most famous for its abundant wildflowers. The small size and remoteness of these islands means that even most Japanese people have never visited them.

You could spend a whole month in Hokkaido (renting a car is a good idea thanks to the somewhat limited public transport network) and not even begin to scratch the surface of what the island has to offer.
Check out (◙ www.en.visit-hokkaido.jp) for more information.

Tohoku

Comprising of the six mountainous prefectures Fukushima, Miyagi, Iwate, Akita, Yamagata and Aomori in northern Honshu, Tohoku is famous for unspoilt nature, glorious hot springs and harsh winters. Much of the east coast (particularly around Sendai) was badly damaged by the March 2011 Great East Japan earthquake and the resulting tsunami which killed over 15,000 people, and the area around the Fukushima Daiichi nuclear plant is still off limits. However, most of the region has now recovered and there is much to see and do for the intrepid traveller, and there are good *shinkansen* links from Tokyo.

In Aomori in the far north is the attractive castle town of **Hirosaki**, while on the western coast are the remote **Shirakami Sanchi** mountains where the last remaining ancient beech forests in Japan are to be found. Akita is renowned for beautiful nature, and the former samurai town of **Kakunodate** is a wonderful cherry blossom spot.

Heading east into Iwate, the **Sanriku Coast** was badly damaged in the earthquake, but its rocky inlets, cliffs and coves are stunningly beautiful, and tourism is vital to continue the revitalisation of the area. Yamagata has many great *onsen* (hot spring baths), and **Mt. Zao** is an active volcano with a stunning crater lake and great skiing in the winter. Miyagi's capital is **Sendai** (the largest city in the Tohoku region), and nearby **Matsushima** is a picturesque bay full of pine-clad rocky islets, home to one of Japan's three famous scenic views. Closer to Tokyo in Fukushima prefecture, **Aizu** is an attractive small city with a samurai history, and **Mt. Bandai** is popular for hiking and skiing.
See (◙ www.en.tohokukanko.jp) for lots more information.

Western Japan

Referred to as the *Chugoku* region (which confusingly translates as 'middle country', owing to it being the main area of settlement in ancient times) the western part of Honshu has a number of places of interest. On the *Seto* Inland Sea coast is **Hiroshima** (see previous chapter for details of visiting as a daytrip from Kansai), the scene of the world's first nuclear attack during WWII. **Okayama** is home to Korakuen, one of Japan's most famous gardens, while at the far western tip of Honshu lies **Yamaguchi**, a hilly prefecture with a historical capital city of the same name.

The northern coast (*San-In*) is much more rural, full of windy coastal roads and charming villages. **Mt. Daisen**, close to the town of Yonago, is the highest peak in the region and great for hiking in summer, while the samurai town of **Matsue** has bundles of history.

Shikoku

The smallest of Japan's four main islands, Shikoku is mostly rural and mountainous, and until the building of three huge bridges to the mainland in the last few decades was only accessible by boat. On the island's west side, **Matsuyama** is Shikoku's largest city which is overlooked by a fine hilltop castle, and the nearby Dogo Onsen is one of Japan's oldest hot spring resorts.

The remote **Iya Valley** deep in the island's mountainous interior is well-known for its steep rocky gorges which can only be crossed by traditional vine bridges. Close to Tokushima city on the eastern side of Shikoku are the **Naruto Whirlpools** which form in the narrow sea strait, and can be viewed from boats which sail daringly close to them. Naruto is also the start point for the Shikoku Pilgrimage; an ancient route which circles the island, taking in 88 sacred temples over the course of about 40 days.

Kyushu

Japan's third largest island is a land of volcanoes, hot springs and friendly people, with a climate that is generally milder than most of Honshu. In the north is **Fukuoka**, Kyushu's most lively city with its open air food stalls (*yatai*), exciting nightlife and the famous Hakata ramen (pork based *tonkotsu*-style). Further west is the port of **Nagasaki**, the second city to be devastated by a nuclear bomb, but also a city which had great significance for trade relations when Japan first opened up to the world. It is an attractive place to visit, with lots to see and do.

To the east in Oita prefecture is the bubbling hot spring city of **Beppu** with its range of hot baths, mud baths, sand baths and colourful hot springs (not all for bathing). The nearby hot spring resort town of **Yufuin** is a scenic getaway sitting in the shadow of Mt. Yufu. Sitting proudly in the centre of Kyushu, **Mt. Aso** is one of the largest volcanic calderas in the world, the centre of which is still very active and currently off-limits. Nearby

Kumamoto is an attractive city with one of the most noteworthy castles in Japan.

Further south, **Miyazaki** has gained a reputation for good surfing, while the city of **Kagoshima** lies in the shadow of Sakurajima just across the bay, an extremely active volcano that regularly covers the city in a layer of ash. Lying off the southern tip of Kyushu are a number of inhabited islands, the most famous of which is **Yakushima**, a mountainous and thickly forested wilderness home to ancient cedar trees and wildlife such as deer, monkeys and sea turtles.

Okinawa and the Southwest Islands

Another side of Japan completely, the islands of Okinawa and the Nansei-Shoto (Southwest Islands) stretch for some 1000km from the southern tip of Kyushu all the way to Yonaguni-jima, just 100km from Taiwan. White beaches, coral reefs, balmy temperatures and a laidback lifestyle mean the islands have a unique feel all of their own. The region's biggest city is Naha on the main island of **Okinawa**, and it is here you can find good food and nightlife (and a big expat scene thanks to the US military presence). The rest of the island has many places of cultural and historical interest (many related to WWII), with some of the best beaches and scenic areas located further north.

Heading south across the island chain, **Ishigaki** (◙ www.ishigaki-japan.com) has many beautiful beaches with crystal clear waters perfect for snorkelling and scuba diving. Just a short ferry ride away is **Taketomi**, a small island where time seems to have stood still amongst a landscape of ox-drawn carts and dry stone walls made from coral. At the very western frontier of Japan is **Iriomote** Island, a sub-tropical natural paradise of steamy rainforests and rare wildlife.

10. When to visit

Japan has a wide range of climates, from the sub-arctic extremes of northern Hokkaido, to the subtropical paradise of Okinawa, so deciding on when is best to visit largely depends on where exactly you intend to visit. However, assuming our itinerary is mostly focused in and around the big cities of Honshu (namely Tokyo and Kyoto), then it is much easier to make a plan.

As most Japanese people will rejoice in telling you, mainland Japan has four distinct seasons (spring, summer, autumn, winter) and a month-long rainy season starting in early June. **Spring** generally lasts from mid-March until late May, and is widely regarded as the best time to visit as temperatures are mild and pleasant. It is also the famous **cherry blossom season** (known as *hanami*), when for two weeks everywhere is pink and beautiful, people gather in parks and in outdoor areas to drink, eat and be merry and there is a real festival atmosphere. The cherry blossom sweeps across the country from the south to north (Okinawa is in bloom from January!), but you can usually count on it being in full bloom around the last week of March/early April in central Honshu.
Check (◙ www.jnto.go.jp/sakura/eng/index.php) for up-to-date cherry blossom forecasts.

There are many **national holidays** in Japan, which are listed on the following website,

(◉ www.timeanddate.com/holidays/japan) but shops and attractions tend to remain open. Some attractions may usually be closed on a Monday, but if this happens to be a national holiday then they will be closed on the Tuesday instead (always worth checking beforehand).

Around a month or so after *hanami* season is **Golden Week** (early May); a series of consecutive national holidays which sees a mass exodus of people leaving the big cities to visit every far-flung corner of Japan, with resulting accommodation and travel woes. Tourist attractions everywhere are often busy and hotel prices increase dramatically, while roads get clogged up and trains can be packed, so try to avoid any long trips on public transport at that time.

Early June is the start of **rainy season**, and this usually lasts until early July. Some years can be extremely wet, with heavy rain almost a daily occurrence, while other years can be surprisingly dry or just predominantly cloudy, with occasional rain showers and frequent sunny days. Even so, you will rarely find Japanese people planning big hiking trips at this time, so if you are willing to gamble with the weather, it could be a good time to explore the great outdoors without the big crowds.

Summer really kicks in from mid-July, lasting all the way through to mid-September, with temperatures frequently over 30 degrees Celsius and extremely high humidity. Being outdoors for any length of time can be very sweaty and uncomfortable, but this is also the main festival season, with evening fireworks displays and traditional parades of all kinds (for more details of festivals see the next chapter).

From the end of September until early December, the cooler temperatures and the changing colours of the leaves make **autumn** a good time to visit. In recent years, a few consecutive national holidays have been bunched together to form a 'Silver Week', where once again people seize the chance to travel at both home and abroad. Things tend not to be as busy as the earlier Golden Week, but it's worth remembering that prices and seats may be at a premium again.

Winter is from mid-December until early March, and temperatures can be exceedingly cold, but it is often dry. It can snow occasionally in Tokyo, but is fairly uncommon in Kyoto, and very rare in Osaka. Outside of the big cities however, it is fairly typical for places to be blanketed in snow for most of the winter, and the north coast of Japan gets some of the heaviest snowfall in the world, as frigid air blows in off the Sea of Japan, often dumping metres of the white stuff. The larger mountains of central Honshu, as well as much of Tohoku and Hokkaido are often snow-covered until early summer. In the cities, everything continues much as normal, so visiting

in winter is not a problem, but in more rural areas, shops and attractions may be closed or have shorter opening hours, and public transport often runs on more limited schedules.
Winter does see a lot of fine and sunny days, particularly in the big cities on Japan's Pacific side (Tokyo, Kyoto, Osaka), so as long as you wrap up warm, it can in fact be a very good time to visit.

In summary, for the most stable weather and pleasant temperatures conducive to sightseeing, spring and autumn are generally the best times to visit, and winter sees many fine (but cold) days.

Cherry blossom (*sakura*) in full bloom

11. Festivals

Festivals (*matsuri*) *are* a huge part of life in Japan, and almost every shrine has one of its own. As there are a lot of shrines in Japan, this means a lot of festivals, both big and small, some quiet and solemn, most lively and loud! The summer is generally festival season, but they take place throughout the year, and stumbling across a small local festival involving the whole community in jovial mood is one of the great joys of being in Japan.

Most festivals are held to celebrate a shrine's deity, or for some seasonal or historical event. There are often processions where the *kami* (deity) is carried through the streets, or decorated *dashi* (floats) are pulled by chanting locals accompanied by the beat of drums.

There are far too many festivals to list here, so what follows are a selection of the most famous ones. See (◙ www.japan-guide.com/event) for more detailed up-to-date information.

Early February - Sapporo Snow Festival – A week of snow and ice sculptures in the city's Odori Park.

March 1st-14th - Omizutori (Nara) – A festival-like period of Buddhist ceremonies, including the nightly burning of torches on the balcony of the impressive (and wooden!) Todaiji Temple.

May 15th – Aoi Matsuri (Kyoto) – A large parade of people in Heian period aristocratic costumes marching between the Imperial Palace and Kamo Shrine.

Around May 15th – Kanda Matsuri (Tokyo) – One of Japan's top three festivals. A week of various events spread across central Tokyo and local neighbourhoods.

Mid-May – Sanja Matsuri (Tokyo) – Another of Tokyo's big festivals, held at Asakusa Shrine.

July – Gion Matsuri (Kyoto) – Second of the three most famous festivals in Japan, featuring a parade of impressively-tall street floats.

July 25th – Tenjin Matsuri (Osaka) – Rounding off the top three festivals, this one features street parades, boats lit-up on the river and a huge fireworks display.

October 22nd – Jidai Matsuri (Kyoto) – A large scale historical parade stretching from the Imperial Palace to the Heian Shrine.

12. Getting to and from the airport

Narita International Airport

Narita International airport is Tokyo's main airport (the other being Haneda), and it is located about an hour away from the city in the surprisingly rural but neighbouring Chiba prefecture. There are two main ways to reach Tokyo from Narita; by bus or by train (there are also taxis for the super-rich!). The various options are as follows:

Bus

Limousine bus - 3,100 yen one way/4,500 yen return - departs for various inner-city hotels
(◉ www.limousinebus.co.jp/en)

Tokyo Shuttle bus – 900 yen with reservation/1000 yen otherwise - goes to Tokyo station
(◉ www.keiseibus.co.jp/kousoku)

The Access Narita bus – 1000 yen one way – drops off at Tokyo and Ginza stations
(◉ www.accessnarita.jp/en/home)

The Narita Shuttle – 1000 yen one way – operates between Narita and Osaki on the JR Yamanote Line, so useful for those using JR trains or going on to Yokohama

(◙ www.willerexpress.com/en/airport-
shuttle/narita-shuttle)

Train

Regular train – about 1,200 yen – take the Keisei
Line (note this is not a JR line) and change at
Nippori for the JR Yamanote Line
(◙ www.hyperdia.com)

Sky Access Express train – about 1,400 yen –
good for some of the inner-city subway lines
(◙ www.www.keisei.co.jp/keisei/tetudou/
skyliner/us/index.php)

Skyliner train – 2,470 yen (cheaper if reserved
online) – super quick, only 36 minutes to Nippori
(◙ www.keisei.co.jp/keisei/tetudou/skyliner/us/
index.php)

Narita Express – 4000 yen return – good value,
as you can travel a relatively long distance on it,
and less busy or stressful than the regular trains
(◙ www.jreast.co.jp/e/pass/nex_round.html)

Insider tip:

- If you plan on using your JR Pass straight away
then you can activate it at Narita, but if you plan
on staying in Tokyo for a few days at first, then it
may be worthwhile investing in a Pasmo or
Suica card from the JR ticket office; they are top-

up cards for use on all trains, subways, buses and even in some shops (costs 500 yen for the card plus the amount you wish to charge it with).

Haneda Airport

Formerly known as Tokyo International Airport, Haneda Airport is only 30 minutes south of central Tokyo, making it much closer to the city than Narita. However it mostly handles domestic flights these days, although a number of international flights are also regularly scheduled, but often at very inconvenient times in the early morning or late at night.
There are a number of easy ways to get to and from the airport.

Tokyo Monorail

This connects Haneda Airport with Hamamatsucho station on the JR Yamanote Line, and so is very convenient for many locations around Tokyo. It only takes 20 minutes and costs 490 yen. It is also fully covered by the JR Rail Pass and an assortment of other JR passes.

Keikyu Railways

Keikyu Railways connects Haneda Airport with Shinagawa station in Tokyo and also the Asakusa subway line. It takes only 15 minutes and costs 410 yen. This is not covered by the JR Rail Pass, but Keikyu offer their own discount tickets for arriving visitors which combine the train ride to Tokyo with day passes for the subway lines by Tokyo Metro and Toei, so are something to consider.

Limousine Bus

A number of bus companies offer connections to various places in Tokyo, including many of the major hotels. Prices can be anywhere from 620 to 2000 yen, depending on destination and time, but the buses tend to run earlier and later than the trains and monorail (typically from 4.30am to around 1am) so are a good option for late or early arrivals.

Taxis

Lastly, there are always taxis, but these will cost at least 5000 yen into central Tokyo, and there is a 20% surcharge at night. If you have a very early or late flight then it may be wise to stay at a hotel near the airport, as trains and most buses stop running at around midnight.

Some nearby hotels include Royal Park Hotel The Haneda (in the International Terminal), Haneda Excel Hotel Tokyu (Terminal 2) and First Cabin Tokyo Haneda (a capsule hotel at Terminal 1). There are other hotels near Otorii and Anamori-Inari stations, but they require a short 1500 yen taxi ride if the trains aren't running.

Kansai International Airport (Osaka)

Another popular point of entry into Japan, Kansai Airport is located some 40km south of central Osaka, and is built on a manmade island in Osaka Bay. The airport handles many international and domestic flights.
There is also the smaller Itami Airport in north Osaka which these days handles mostly domestic flights.
The main options connecting Kansai Airport and the city are:

JR Trains

The JR Haruka Limited Express - runs between the airport and Tennoji in the south of the city (30 minutes, 1710 yen unreserved / 2200 yen reserved seat) and Shin-Osaka (for bullet train connections) in the north (50 minutes, 2330 yen unreserved / 3000 yen reserved).
If you intend to buy an Icoca card (see next chapter) it may be worth purchasing an 'Icoca & Haruka' special combination tourist ticket which will save you money on unreserved seats on the Haruka train.

JR Kansai Airport Rapid train – is a little slower but a bit cheaper and connects the airport to

Tennoji (50 minutes, 1060 yen) and Osaka station (70 minutes, 1190 yen).

Both the JR trains are of course covered by the JR Rail Pass (which can be activated at Kansai Airport), but only for unreserved seats on the Haruka.

Nankai Railways

The Nankai 'Rap:t' Limited Express – these trains go to and from Nankai Namba station in about 35 minutes (1430 yen, all reserved). There are also slightly slower and cheaper Nankai express trains which take 45 minutes (920 yen). If you intend to transfer to the subway at Namba, the consider the 'Kanku Chikatoku Ticket', which combines the train ride from the airport to Namba with a journey to any subway station within Osaka for only 1000 yen (available the other way too).

Limousine Bus

Many bus companies run to various places in Osaka, Kyoto and beyond, including the main train stations and hotels. They typically take about an hour to central Osaka and cost from around 1000 to 1500 yen. Go to the bus terminal at the airport or ask at your hotel for details.

Travelling onwards to Kyoto - Kyoto is about an hour and half from Kansai International airport. There are many trains from JR Osaka station to Kyoto, taking about 30 to 40 minutes. The JR Limited Express 'Haruka' runs directly from the airport to Kyoto station every 30 mins (2850 yen non-reserved).

There are also frequent airport buses which take around 100 mintes.

(◙ www.okkbus.co.jp/en/timetable/kix/f_kyt.html ¥2550)

13. Rail Passes

The JR Rail Pass

The JR pass is available to anyone visiting the country on a tourist visa, and it saves a lot of money when travelling around. Japan Rail (JR) is the national rail network and so covers the entire country, and includes the *shinkansen* (bullet train). Unless you are staying in Japan for only two or three days or only planning to stay in one city, then a JR pass is a must.

To be eligible for a JR pass, you must be a visitor from a foreign country entering Japan for sightseeing reasons, with the corresponding 'temporary visitor' stamp in your passport (which you'll receive upon arrival at immigration). Japanese nationals living abroad may also be eligible (see the website for details).

There are two types of JR pass on offer, ordinary or green (allows use of the premium green cars), and these are available for durations of 7-days, 14-days or 21-days. Prices for children are roughly half those of adults. Full details can be found on the JR rail pass website.
(◙ www.japanrailpass.net/en/about_jrp.html)

Ordinary JR Pass (adult)

7-days – 29,110 yen
14-days – 46,390 yen
21-days – 59,350 yen

Green JR Pass (adult)

7-days – 38,880 yen
14-days – 62,950 yen
21-days – 81,870 yen

The green pass allows for travel in the superior-class green cars, which along with the slightly extra luxury, can often have free seats available during busy periods. But for most people, the ordinary pass should be just fine. Also be aware that although prices are listed in yen, you **must buy your JR pass before arriving** in Japan.

The JR pass is valid for travel on all JR trains (and JR buses and ferries), including the *shinkansen* (bullet train). However it is **not valid** for the Nozomi or Mizuho *shinkansen* trains (which have fewer stops and so have slightly faster journey times), but all other bullet trains are perfectly fine. All classes of *shinkansen* trains are very frequent, so there are not any issues here.

To purchase a JR pass, buy an 'exchange order' from a designated sales office or agent in your country **before coming to Japan.** Search the internet for reputable agents or check

(◙ www.japanrailpass.net/en/purchase.html) for lists of sellers.

When you arrive in Japan, you must turn in your 'exchange order' along with your passport at the Japan Rail Pass exchange office at any major JR station (which include Narita Airport, Tokyo, Shinjuku, Shibuya, Kansai Airport, Osaka and Kyoto stations). You will then be presented with your JR pass and are free to use it from that point on for its full duration. Be aware that your 'exchange pass' must be turned in for a JR pass within three months of the date of purchase, so don't buy one too far ahead of your trip's starting date.

To use your JR pass, don't enter the automatic ticket gates at stations, but simply show your pass at a staff attended gate. You can also go to the reservation office (*midori-no-guchi*) to reserve seats ahead of time.

So should you buy a JR pass? The answer is a resounding YES! When you consider that the average price of a one-way *shinkansen* ticket between Tokyo and Kyoto is around 13,000 yen, then a single trip to Kyoto and back costs almost the same as a 7-day JR pass. So for 7 days of unlimited travel all over the country, it really can be a huge money saver and very convenient too. It is not valid for the various subway lines or private railways (of which there are many), but it is possible to see much of Tokyo using only the JR

Yamanote line. In the Kansai area, Osaka has its own inner-city JR loop line and all the main cities (Kyoto, Osaka, Nara, Kobe etc) are connected by JR lines, so even if you're only planning a few daytrips it is a very worthwhile investment and highly recommended.

See (◙ www.japanrailpass.net/en/index.html) for all the rail pass information you need.

Other Rail Passes

There are a whole variety of other rail passes available which cover certain cities or areas, allow travel on railways or subway lines not covered by the JR pass, or that include entry or discounts to attractions and travel. It is certainly worthwhile searching online for the area you will be in to see what is on offer.

Regional Passes

JR East have a number of region specific passes which may suit your needs if you don't intend to travel right across the country, or have a few days before or after your main JR Pass has activated/expired (◙ www.jreast.co.jp/e/pass). Likewise, **JR West** have a variety of passes ranging from 1-day to a week, covering specific areas (◙ www.westjr.co.jp/global/en/ticket/pass).

There are a bewildering number of city specific passes, such as the Tokyo Free Kippu (1590 yen) which allows unlimited use of subway lines (Toei and Tokyo Metro) and JR trains in central Tokyo for one full day, but they can be a little pricey, difficult to know what exactly is covered and are probably not worthwhile unless you're on the trains almost all day. For Tokyo, prepaid IC cards are the best way to go (see next part).

Prepaid IC Cards

These don't give you any discounts, but they provide convenience as you can ride almost any train or bus (JR, subways, other train lines) in the city, and can even be used to pay for items in many shops.
IC cards can be purchased at ticket machines or ticket counters for a refundable deposit of 500 yen, plus an initial amount to be charged onto the card. You can then top-up the cards at machines as and when you need to. To use them, just touch the card onto the reader as you pass through an automatic ticket gate; your current balance will flash up on the small screen too.

Different cities and regions have separate IC cards, but since 2013, Japan's most popular cards were made compatible, so you can now use just one card wherever you go in the country.
Suica is the prepaid IC card by JR East in Tokyo and Tohoku, while Pasmo is the card of Tokyo's other rail, subway and bus operators (but all are

interchangeable). Icoca is the repaid IC card for JR in Western Japan, while Toica is the central (Nagoya and Shizuoka version). Other cities and regions have their own versions too, but all function in much the same way.

Insider tips:

- As ever, (◉ www.hyperdia.com) is the best website for checking train times and connections.

- Once you have your rail passes sorted, be sure to download the very useful NAVITIME for Japan Travel app. It can help you with getting around, has detailed route maps, shows train and bus timetables and you can even search for free Wi-Fi spots when offline.
(◉ www.navitimejapan.com).

14. Internet and Wi-Fi

In this day and age it seems that everyone must be 'connected' twenty-four seven, and long gone are the days when going on a trip effectively meant cutting yourself off from the world. Whatever way you look at it, the internet has changed travelling forever and now people feel lost if they can't check information online, use maps apps or keep up with social media. Luckily in recent years Japan has really moved forward with regards to Wi-Fi access and options, and now travellers have many ways to get online while on the road.

Free Wi-Fi

Many establishments offer free Wi-Fi for just entering the premises; it's usually just a matter of connecting to the Wi-Fi network on your smartphone, tablet or other device. Well-known international chains such as MacDonald's and Starbucks are the best examples, but many other coffee shops, cafes and stores also have free Wi-Fi, so just lookout for the signs plastered around.

Yodobashi Camera is a huge department chain store selling all kinds of goods and also offers many perks to foreign visitors, including free Wi-Fi and tax exemptions on purchased goods (always have your passport with you as you'll need to show it).

Also be sure to check at tourist spots, train stations, bus stops, convenience stores (especially 7-Eleven and Family Mart), tourist information offices and airports as many of these offer free Wi-Fi access too (you may occasionally need to signup to something beforehand). Most hotels also have free Wi-Fi for staying guests, and so if you are planning on spending most of your time in the big cities, then random free Wi-Fi spots may be all you need during your trip.

Another good tip is to search online for free Wi-Fi in the city you'll be staying in, and there are some useful apps such as NAVITIME for Japan Travel which allow you to search for Wi-Fi hotspots, even when offline.

Pre-paid SIM cards

These are another good option if using a smartphone, as they allow you to stay online when you are on the move, which is very useful, especially if you intend to use online maps to navigate around.

Make sure your phone is unlocked first, and purchase a visitor SIM card at the airport or from any of the big electronic stores such as Yodobashi Camera, Softmap etc. Staff in these stores can often speak a smattering of English (or will find someone who can), and they will help advise on size of SIM card (mini, micro, nano) and best service providers (such as b-mobile, Docomo, AU or Softbank). Prices can start from as low as 2500 yen, but it varies depending on coverage, duration and data usage.

A popular SIM card is PAYG SIM by b-mobile, which provides 3GB of data for seven days at 9980 yen. This includes 60 minutes of calls, has good coverage across Japan and is more than enough data for a week.
A cheaper option would be the Japan Travel SIM by IIJmio, which provides 2GB for 90 days for only 3790 yen.

Pocket Wi-Fi

These are popular options for people who want to connect whilst on the move, and use Wi-Fi across multiple devices. It does mean carrying (and charging) yet another device, but they are cheap to rent and very reliable (as long as the battery doesn't run out!).

There are many options out there, including (◉ www.japanwifibuddy.com) who can set you up with everything you need; order before your trip for pickup at the airport or your hotel and connect right away. Prices from about 4200 yen (£26/$39) for a week.
The device comes with a prepaid envelope which means that you can mail it back at the end

of your trip (either from the airport post office or your hotel may even take care of this if you ask nicely).

Other popular and reliable providers include:
Japan Wireless
(◙ www.japan-wireless.com)

Global Advanced Communications
(◙ www.globaladvancedcomm.com/
pocketwifi.html)

Many Airbnb accommodations will provide a free pocket Wi-Fi device for guests to use during their stay, so it might be worth checking this with the owners before you arrive.

Internet cafes

Once the favourite haunts of travellers in Japan, internet cafes or '*manga kissa*' as they are colloquially known (abbreviated from *manga-kissaten*, or 'comic cafes') are possibly less popular with foreign visitors than they used to be, due to the proliferation of Wi-Fi hot spots in the big cities.
These net cafes are typically open 24 hours a day, and offer a small space to work, read, rest or sleep for a few hours, or indeed all night. Spaces range from small partitioned desks with a workstation and internet access, to slightly larger (and more expensive) private cubicles

with reclining chairs, sofas or soft floors to lie down on. There are also often shower facilities (useful for hung-over salary men with work the next day), food vending machines and free drinks and ice-cream.

Most internet cafes charge for a fixed number of hours, and then you'll pay extra for additional use after that. There are also frequently flat rates for all day (or night) usage. Prices are usually low; expect to pay from as little as 200 yen for an hour, going up to around 3000 yen for 12 hours and use of the showers.

Internet/manga cafes are frequently found around train stations; it's usually best to look for the big '24hr' signs on the building. Some of the popular big chains include MediaCafe Popeye, Manboo, or Gran Cyber Café.

15. Japan Do's and Don'ts

Japan is a warm and welcoming country to foreign visitors, and with the government equipping itself to cope with the increased number of tourists expected to arrive in the years leading up to the Tokyo Olympics in 2020, there has never been a better time to visit. However, Japan is also a country steeped in tradition and etiquette, which can sometimes be bewildering for those unused to its subtleties.
So to do things the Japanese way (and to avoid committing any social faux-pas), here are a few tips for your stay.

Eating

Slurp your noodles, it helps to cool them if they're hot. In fact, you can slurp just about any food here, it won't be considered rude.

Don't play with your chopsticks. Also, don't leave them upstanding in a bowl of rice, or pass food from one person's chopsticks to another; both are associated with practices at funerals.

No tipping at restaurants (or anywhere else for that matter).

At the end of the meal, you can ask for the cheque, or say '*o-kaikei-kudasai*', to get the bill.

It is usual to pay at the cash register after the meal (although at some ramen places etc there is a machine to select and pay for your meal upfront).

Money

Japan is a cash-based society, and although many shops and hotels take credit cards these days, don't always assume that they will (especially in more out of the way places).

Many ATMs don't accept foreign cards, apart from ATMs at post offices and 7-eleven stores, so use those.

ATMs at 7-eleven stores operate 24 hours a day, but ones at post offices have limited operating hours, so plan accordingly.

It's generally very safe to carry cash around, and it's always a good idea to have some on you.

Footwear

Many places require you to remove your shoes before entry, especially if there is a sunken-foyer entrance (*genkan*).

Neatly leave your shoes there (facing outwards), or put them on the shelf or in the shoe locker if there is one.

Always remove shoes when entering someone's house.

When going to the bathroom, toilet slippers should be used and returned to the exact spot you found them.

It pays to always wear nice clean socks (no holes!)

Shrines

Be quiet and respectful.

Most shrines have a water source for use before entering, so use the ladle to pour water over your hands to rinse them.

To make a prayer, put a money offering in the box, clap twice, bow twice, quietly make your prayer, bow again, take one step backwards while facing the shrine, then turn around to leave. If there is a gong of some type, use it before praying to get the deity's attention.

In public

When riding trains (or other forms of transport), try not to talk too loudly.

Train platforms have markings to show where to queue.

Don't blow your nose in public; find a quiet corner to do so.

People tend not to eat while walking (although this is probably slowly changing, and goes out of the window during festivals!).

Train stations

Don't forget that these can be a great source of information when you first reach your destination; most train stations (even small, unassuming ones) often have a Tourist Information Centre or counter, so head there for free maps and advice on things to do, places to eat, places to stay etc.

There are usually always lockers for storing your stuff, and most bus stops are right next to the station.

16. Must-eat foods

Japanese cuisine has a reputation for high quality and often subtle flavours, but one of its most notable qualities is the huge variety of dishes to be found. Many of these (such as sushi or *katsu*-curry) are increasingly well-known abroad, but even so, the quality tends to be much higher in Japan itself. Most restaurants specialise in a certain kind of dish, so it helps to know what you are looking for.
Izakayas (Japanese pubs) and *shokudo* (all-round restaurants) offer a variety of dishes and are generally good value, but it pays to visit a speciality restaurant for the best food experience.

It would be impossible to list all the dishes you should try here, but what follows is a selection of Japanese staples from across the broad spectrum of Japanese cuisine.

Sushi and sashimi

Sushi consists of cooked vinegar-laced rice with various other ingredients either balanced on top, or rolled up inside. These can include seafood (often raw), *nori* (seaweed), vegetables and other less traditional items such as avocado, hamburgers and fruit. Sashimi is sliced raw fish (or meat) which is served without rice. Both sushi and sashimi are well known abroad, but are probably eaten less frequently by Japanese people than most foreigners would expect.

Sushi-ya are specialist sushi restaurants where customers sit at tables or at the counter, and the chefs prepare each order as it comes. *Kaitenzushi* are the famous conveyor belt sushi restaurants, where customers are free to take dishes as they trundle past their table, before all the plates are counted up at the end and the bill is calculated. They tend to be cheaper than traditional sushi restaurants.

Seaside towns usually have the most sushi restaurants, but here are some good places to eat sushi in the main cities:

Tokyo – Head to any of the restaurants in Tsukiji fish market's outer market before midday (most close in the afternoon) to take your pick of some of the freshest fish in the capital.

Kyoto – Sushi Iwa – Premium option close to Kyoto station, chef speaks English, prices for one piece start at 500 yen, a course is around 10,000 yen.
(☒ www.sushiiwa.jp/en ☼ 12pm-2pm/5pm-10pm/closed Mondays, ¥2000-30000, 600-8155)

Osaka – Yakko Sushi – Affordable sushi, from 90 yen a plate!
(☒ www.battera.co/k00122 ☼ 12pm-10pm/closed Thursdays, ¥90-1500, 530-0022)

Ramen

Ramen is a noodle-based dish, consisting of Chinese-style wheat noodles in a meat (or occasionally) fish based broth. It is often flavoured with soy sauce or miso, and served with toppings such as sliced pork (*tonkotsu*), soft boiled eggs (*nitamago*) and spring onions (*negi*).

Ramen is a cheap and hearty meal (don't forget to slurp!), and every region has its own variation on the dish.

Look out for ramen restaurants by spotting the ラーメン characters on signs, they are everywhere. In some places you must use a machine to place your order up front; insert your money, choose your dish and side-orders, and hand the ticket over to the staff.

Ramen restaurants really can be found everywhere, so just pop in to wherever looks (or smells) good.
Also check out (◉ www.ramenadventures.com) for lots of great information and ramen shop recommendations.
Here are some good ones in the big ramen cities:

Tokyo – <u>Menya Musashi</u> – Famous Tokyo-style *shoyu* ramen, many branches around the city, but Shinjuku is the flagship.
(☼ 11am-10.30pm, ¥500-2000, 160-0023)

Kyoto – <u>Menyakisshoumaru </u> – Great ramen in rich broth, in a small place between Shijo and Sanjo Dori on the narrow Kiya-machi Dori, parallel to the river. (☼ 12pm-12am, ¥600-1500)

Osaka – Ramen Kio – Hearty ramen in the lively Dotonbori area
(☼ 11.30am-4.30am, ¥500-2000, 542-0071)

Fukuoka – Ramen Taizo – Fukuoka-style *tonkotsu* ramen.
(☼ 12pm-3.15am/closed Sundays, ¥500-2000, 812-0018)

Udon

Udon is a thick wheat-flour noodle, served in a hot (or cold) broth made from *dashi*, soy sauce and *mirin*. Toppings can include scallions (*negi*), tempura (often prawn) and a slice of fish-cake (*kamaboko*). Again, there are many regional varieties, the main differences being the broth (light or dark) or the toppings.
Udon is cheap (around 300 yen for a basic bowl) and a slightly healthier option than ramen.

Marugame Seimen is a popular chain with restaurants all over the country (over 65 in Tokyo alone), but the quality is high and the prices are cheap.
(◙ www.toridoll.com/en/shop/marugame)

Here are some other good udon restaurant options:

Tokyo – <u>Sanukiya</u> - Michelin-starred udon restaurant.
(◙ www.koenji-sanukiya.com ☼ 6pm-11pm/closed Sundays, ¥800-4000, 166-0003)

Kyoto – <u>Yamamoto Menzo</u> – Always a queue, but it's worth the wait.
(◙ www.eng.trip.kyoto.jp/spot/db/yamamot-omenzou ☼ 11am-7.45pm/2.30pm on Wednesdays, ¥600-2000, 606-8334)

Osaka – <u>Tsurutontan</u> – Big bowls of udon, good value, branches nationwide.
(◙ www.tsurutontan.co.jp ☼ 11am-11pm, ¥800-2500, 542-0084)

Kushikatsu

Kushikatsu is deep fried meat, seafood or vegetables on skewers (*kushi*), which customers dip into a soy-based kushikatsu sauce before eating (only dip once as the dipping sauce is shared by customers).

There are many skewers to choose from, including beef (*gyuniku*), pork (*butaniku*), chicken balls (*tsukune*), squid (*ika*), shrimp (*ebi*), pumpkin (*kabocha*) and *shiitake* mushrooms. It is good fun to order a whole variety and they go great with beer. *Shin-sekai* in Osaka is said to be where the dish originated and is the most famous place in Japan for *kushikatsu*.

Osaka – The Shinsekai neighbourhood of Osaka has countless *kushikatsu* restaurants, so explore the streets around the famous Tsutenkaku tower and take your pick. (5 minutes from JR Shin-Imamiya station / Ebisucho and Dobutsuen-Mae subway)

Tokyo – <u>Kushikatsu Tanaka</u> – Cheap chain serving Osaka-style kushikatsu (◙ www.kushi-tanaka.com (*Japanese*) ☼ 4pm-2am, ¥300-4000, 150-0011)

Yakitori

Another skewer-based dish, but this time it is chicken grilled over a charcoal fire. Various cuts of meat are available and it is usually seasoned with *tare* (a sweetened and thickened soy sauce) or salt. *Yakitori* is often found on *izakaya* menus, but for the best experience, head to a small, hole-in-the-wall *yakitori* restaurant.

Tokyo – Head to Omoide Yokocho (Piss Alley) in Shinjuku for many cheap and good eateries.

Kyoto – <u>Yakitori Tarokichi</u> – Good location close to Gion
(☼ 4pm-12am, ¥300-3000, 605-0075)

Osaka - <u>Ayamura</u> – Michelin-starred yakitori
(☼ 5.30pm-11pm/closed Sundays and national holidays, ¥1000-5000, 553-0003)

Shabu shabu and sukiyaki

Shabu shabu is a kind of healthy hotpot dish where thin slices of meat (usually beef or pork) and vegetables are swirled around in a pot of boiling water and *konbu* (kelp). They are then eaten after dipping in a *ponzu* or sesame sauce. Sukiyaki is similar, but the meat and vegetables are dropped in the pot to simmer slowly in a mixture of soy sauce, sugar and *mirin*, giving them a somewhat sweeter taste. These items are then also usually dipped in a small bowl of raw, beaten eggs just before eating.

Tokyo – <u>Shabuzen Roppongi</u> – Delicious, high-grade cuts of meat with a choice of table seating or tatami rooms
(◉ www.roppongi.shabuzen.jp/en ☼ 4pm-11pm, ¥4000-16,000, 106-0032)

Kyoto – <u>Kyoto Shabuzen</u> – The Gion branch is as good as you'd expect, serves Kobe beef (◉ www.kyoto.shabuzen.jp ☼ 4pm-11pm, ¥3700-12,000, 605-0074)

Osaka – <u>Shabutei</u> – Four branches in the city, all are top quality, and good English website (◉ www.shabutei.co.jp/en ☼ 11am-11pm, ¥1000-10,000, 542-0085)

Yakiniku

Yakiniku literally means 'grilled meat', and it involves customers cooking their own small cuts of meat, along with assorted vegetables, over a charcoal grill. The food is then dipped in *tare* sauce and commonly eaten with white rice and side dishes such as *kimchi* (pickled cabbage).

It is sometimes said that *yakiniku* was introduced from Korea, but it has now become a Japanese dish in its own right.

Tokyo – <u>Ebisu Yakiniku Kintan</u> – Friendly and affordable, about 5000 yen for two sharing (☼ 11.30am-2.30pm/6pm-11pm, ¥2000-6000, 150-0021)

Kyoto – <u>Yakiniku Hiro</u> – High quality meat with a number of branches around the city

(◙ www.yakiniku-hiro.com/english ☼ 5pm-12pm, ¥4000-10,000, 605-0085)

Teppanyaki

Teppanyaki is a general style of Japanese cuisine based on food that is cooked on an iron griddle. The high-end version typically includes *wa-gyu* (premium quality meat, such as the famed Kobe beef), seafood (lobster, abalone and scallops), along with seasonal vegetables all cooked by a chef in front of the customers. These are multi-course meals and are rarely cheap.

The lower-end version of *teppanyaki* features more regional dishes such as *okonomiyaki* (a kind of pancake stuffed with cabbage and a choice of meat or seafood, popular in Osaka), *yakisoba* (fried noodles) or *monjayaki* (the Tokyo version of *okonomiyaki*) all of which are also cooked on a griddle.

High-end *teppanyaki*;

Tokyo – Ginza Ukaitei – Expensive but high quality, seasonal menu
(◙ www.ukai.co.jp/english/ginza ☼ 12am-2pm/5pm-9pm/closed Sundays, ¥7000-30,000, 104-0061)

Kyoto – <u>Mikaku</u> – Small, pricey restaurant in Gion, may be best to book, serves wonderful Kobe beef
(☼ 11.30am-2.30pm/5pm-11.30pm/closed Mondays, ¥12,000-20,000, 605-0079)

Lower-end *teppanyaki* (such as *okonomiyaki*);

Tokyo – Head to Tsukishima station (Oedo and Yurakucho subway lines)) and the nearby Nishinaka street, where there is a high concentration of *monjayaki* (もんじゃ焼き) restaurants.

Osaka – <u>Mizuno</u> – One of the most famous *okonomiyaki* restaurants in Osaka
(◉ www.mizuno-osaka.com ☼ 11am-10pm, ¥800-3000, 542-0071)

Japanese sweets

There are a huge variety of Japanese sweets, many made with either *anko* (red *azuki* bean paste) or *mochi* (pounded rice which has a gel-like consistency). *Macha* (green tea) is a popular flavouring for many kinds of sweets.

Wagashi (Japanese sweets) tend not to be as 'sweet' as their foreign equivalents and are rather more delicate in flavour. There are many traditional 'sweets' shops, particularly in tourist spots.

Some varieties to look out for include;

Daifuku, and the similar *manju* (lightly sweetened *mochi* rice stuffed with *anko*)

Taiyaki (a fish-shaped cake made from sweet batter, with *anko* or other fillings)

Dango (a sweet dumpling made from rice flour which comes in a range of varieties; often served with green tea)

Sakuramochi (pink *mochi* with an *anko* centre, wrapped in a pickled cherry blossom leaf)

Popular Japanese sweets shops can be found in:

Tokyo – Head to Asakusa and check out all the sweets on the Nakamise shopping street

Kyoto – The city is full of places serving traditional sweets, especially around Gion, Higashiyama and Arashiyama

17. Must-do activities

There are so many fascinating places to visit in
Japan, that it is easy to burn yourself out with
non-stop visits to shrines, gardens and famous
landmarks. Equally, as Japan is such a safe
country and relatively crime-free, it is also great
fun to just stroll around, discovering interesting
streets and neighbourhoods, without a fixed goal
in mind (and it is highly recommended that you
take time to do this).
However, there are also some activities which
are quintessentially Japanese, the following of
which are all worth trying to squeeze into your
trip at some point.

Onsen (Hot spring baths)

Thanks to the geothermal nature of its location,
Japan has countless natural hot springs all over
the country, and hot spring baths are a big part
of the culture. They range from outdoor pools
(*rotemburo*) in picturesque settings to inner city
public baths, and while a rare few offer mixed
bathing, most are segregated into male and
female areas. *Ryokans* (Japanese traditional
hotels) sometimes have private baths for
couples or families.

There is a strict hot spring etiquette but it is easy
to follow. In the changing room, take off all of
your clothes (everyone is naked) and put them in

the basket along with your towel. You can take a small towel into the bathing area to protect your modesty. Before entering the bath, wash your body using the showers or washbowls, and be careful to rinse off all the soap. You can now enter the bath (be careful, as the water is often hot) and soak for as long as you like. Your small towel can be used in the bath for modesty, or do as the locals do and put it on your head.

One word of warning for anyone with tattoos; many *onsen* won't allow entry to people with inked skin, mainly because tattoos were closely associated with the *yakuza*. Although this image is slowly changing, and some young Japanese people have tattoos these days, most hot springs and *ryokan* are still very traditional, and so the no-tattoo rule is frequently enforced. Look out for signs which make this explicitly clear, or if in doubt, ask at the counter. Some bathhouses are fine with tattoos, others will make you cover them up with plasters (band-aids) but some will refuse entry full stop.
This website (◉ www.fastjapan.com/en/p112265) lists *onsen* and *ryokan* in and around Tokyo which are OK for people with tattoos.

There are so many hot springs all over Japan that it would take a lifetime to list them all, but you can find many suggestions listed throughout this guidebook. Some of the best hot spring resort towns are:

Kusatsu - 2 hours from Tokyo
(◉ www.kusatsuonsen-international.jp/en)

Hakone - 1 hour from Tokyo
(◉ www.hakone.or.jp/en)

Kinosaki - about 2 hours from Kyoto
(◉ www.visitkinosaki.com)

Karaoke

Karaoke is a Japanese institution, and is the perfect way to while away a few rainy hours or even the whole night! Modern establishments are often large, bright multi-floor buildings, and guests get their own private room in which they can select songs to sing and order food and drink (including alcohol) on touch screen devices. There are usually hundreds of English songs to choose from, and even those who are shy or hate singing usually have fun in the end.

At reception you will be asked to write down how many people and for how long you wish to stay, as well as your name, age and possibly accommodation address or instead asked to show some proof of identity. There may be a few more questions, but it's usually possible to fumble through the process despite the language barrier (or you may get lucky and the staff speak some English).

There is often a free self-service soft drink bar, so help yourself before heading to the room. Ten minutes before your time is up there will be a warning either on screen or by phone, and when you finish simply take your tab to the counter and pay.

Karaoke places are found all over the place, so search for the katakana characters カラオケ on signs. Be careful of entering small karaoke bars, as not only will you have to sing in front of everyone, but they are more expensive and serve a mainly male clientele.

The big establishments to look out for are Jankara, Big Echo, Shidax and Karaokekan.

Shopping

Japan is a paradise for shopping, from the loud 'irrashaimase' (welcome) bellowed by shop staff, to the bright lights and staggering variety of goods on offer, and despite Japan's image as an expensive country, there are occasional bargains to be had.
The country produces some of the world's most well-known electronic goods, but it can often be cheaper to buy back at home, and you can not always be guaranteed of English menus on items such as cameras (Sony and Panasonic are Japanese only), so it pays to do some

research. However, for fashion and for quirky items you can literally shop until you drop.

Look out for 100 yen shops (they have a large 100 yen sign outside) which offer a wide range of household goods, stationary and other assorted items, all of surprisingly good quality considering the low prices.

Train stations often have extensive shopping malls attached to them, and large stores such as Yodabashi Camera offer tax refunds for foreigners who show their passport.
Below are the main shopping districts in the major cities.

Tokyo – Ginza, Shinjuku, Shibuya

Kyoto – Shijo street, Nishiki Market (food-related stalls and shops)

Osaka – Umeda, Namba/Shinsaibashi

Hiking

In a country which is over 70% mountainous, it is no surprise that hiking is something of a national pastime. In the distant past, mountains were strictly the sanctuaries of the gods, and were only climbed by the most devoutly religious pilgrims and ascetics. However, by the *Edo* period (1603-1868), people gradually began climbing mountains for pleasure, and these days it is an activity that is enjoyed by folk of all ages (although pensioners predominate!), with everyone kitted out in all the latest colourful outdoor gear.

There are many top class routes and trails throughout every corner of Japan, and although many of them are out of the scope of this book, see the following comprehensive website (◉ www.japanhike.wordpress.com) for detailed information. For the less adventurous, there are also some pleasant day hikes on the edges of the big cities which can be completed in a few hours, and these easy walks offer a wonderful taste of Japan's natural environment.

There are more details on the following hikes in the relevant chapters of this guide;

Tokyo – Mt. Takao

Near Tokyo – Oze National Park, Nikko National Park

Kyoto – Fushimi Inari

Near Kyoto – Mt. Rokko and 'Rokku Gaaden' (Kobe)

Insider tip:

- For off-the-beaten-track walks, **Walk Japan** (◉ www.walkjapan.com) offer tours which combine both nature and culture, allowing you to discover some truly hidden corners of Japan which most tourists never see.

Sumo

A Japanese form of wrestling and Japan's national sport, Sumo is an ancient pastime in which bouts are short and explosive, with the first wrestler to be pushed out of the ring or to touch any part of the ground (except his feet) the loser. Sumo tournaments last for 15 days, with the higher ranking wrestlers appearing later in the day.
Tickets can be surprisingly expensive (especially ringside seats), but it is a great experience, as food and drink can be taken into the stadium and the action is easy to follow. Tickets go on sale one month before the tournament starts and usually sell out, but there are often a small number of tickets held back for sale on the day. The website (◉ www.buysumotickets.com) can organise tickets in advance for you.

Tournaments are held in Tokyo (January, May and September), Osaka (March), Nagoya (July) and Fukuoka (November).
See (◉ www.sumo.or.jp/en) for more details.

18. Places to stay

There are a wealth of places to stay in Japan, and most travellers these days are used to finding the best deals online at websites such as (◉ www.booking.com) or (◉ www.expedia.com).

As in many corners of the globe, Airbnb (◉ www.airbnb.com) has also taken off in Japan recently, especially in the big cities, and is a good option for those on a budget.

The service in Japanese hotels however is second to none, in part thanks to the famous *omotenashi* (high-level hospitality). Be aware that most places prefer guests to book ahead rather than arrive unannounced.

Ryokans

These are old-style Japanese inns which originated in the *Edo* period (1603-1868). The rooms are typically very traditional with tatami-mats, futons for sleeping, and meals are brought to the room and consist of many exquisite courses. *Ryokans* often have hot spring baths, and while they are not usually a cheap option, it is worth staying in one for at least one night to experience a slice of Japanese culture and to enjoy the wonderful service and hospitality.

Check (◙ www.ryokan.or.jp/english) or
(◙ www.japaneseguesthouses.com) for some
good information and suggestions.

Tokyo

Homeikan - old-fashioned style in central Tokyo
(◙ www.homeikan.com ¥from 6500 yen per
person, 113-0033)

Ryokan Kamogawa Asakusa - located in one of
Tokyo's most historic districts
(◙ www.f-kamogawa.jp/english ¥from 8000 yen
per person, 111-0032)

Kyoto

Tawaraya - traditional, homely feel.
(◙ www.ryokan.or.jp/english/yado/main/58900
¥from 30,000 yen per person, 604-8094)

Tamahan - beautiful *ryokan* in Gion district.
(◙ www.tamahan.jp ¥from 20,000 yen per
person, 605-0825)

Hoshinoya - idyllic riverside *ryokan* with all the
trappings of a high-class hotel in peaceful
Arashiyama, accessed by private boat.
(◙ www.hoshinoyakyoto.jp/en ¥from 30,000 yen
per person, 616-0007)

Osaka

Many suggestions at (◙ www.osaka-ryokan.com/lg_en/ryokan/index.html)

Capsule hotels

For a cheap and unique experience, try a night in a capsule hotel. Rooms are small body-length pods with just enough room to sleep in and come with a built in TV, wireless internet and a curtain for a door. Some have separate male and female areas. Luggage is stored in lockers, and there are communal bathrooms. It's a basic setup, but great for those on a tight budget!

Tokyo

Shinjuku Kuyakusho-Mae Capsule Hotel - useful location near station
(◙ www.capsuleinn.com/shinjuku/en ¥from 2000 yen, 160-0021)

Anshin Oyado - many branches very close to popular stations
(◙ www.anshin-oyado.jp/english ¥from 5000 yen, 101-0021)

Kyoto

Capsule Ryokan Kyoto - near Kyoto station, unique tatami capsules
(◉ www.capsule-ryokan-kyoto.com ¥from 4000 yen, 600-8226)

Nine Hours Kyoto - sleek design, close to Gion and Kawaramachi
(◉ www.ninehours.co.jp/en/kyoto ¥from 4900 yen, 600-8031)

Osaka

Asahi Plaza Shinsaibashi - great location, late check-in
(◉ www.asahiplaza.co.jp/capcel/english.html ¥from 3000 yen, 542-0086)

Business hotels

As in any other developed country, business hotels can be found almost everywhere with the lower end ones offering affordable, if functional rooms. In Japan they tend to be located close to train stations, so are very convenient for travellers. Rooms can sometimes smell a bit of old cigarette smoke, so try asking for a non-smoking one (*kinen room* in Japanese).

Tokyo

<u>Tokyu Stay Shibuya</u> - convenient location, but not the cheapest
(◉ www.tokyustay.co.jp/e/hotel/SIB ¥from 10,000 yen, 150-0045)

<u>Sakura Hotel Hatagaya</u> - affordable hotel in a quiet part of Shinjuku
(◉ www.sakura-hotel-hatagaya.com ¥from 7000 yen, 151-0072)

Kyoto

<u>Dormy Inn Kyoto</u> - near the station, has outdoor bath
(¥from 9000 yen, 600-8216)

Osaka

<u>Hotel Kinki</u> - modern hotel in Umeda
(◉ www.hotelkinki.com/en ¥from 3300 yen, 530-0027)

<u>Ibis Styles Osaka</u> - pleasant hotel in lively Dotonbori area
(◉ www.ibis.com ¥from 8000 yen, 542-0084)

Luxury hotels

There are a wide range of luxurious, top-end hotels in the bigger cities, offering the very best in terms of accommodation, food, hospitality and facilities. Be aware, that it is often customary to pay an extra fee to use amenities such as the swimming pool, gym or spa.

Tokyo

Ritz-Carlton Tokyo - one of the top 5-star hotels in Tokyo
(◉ www.ritzcarlton.com/en/hotels/japan/tokyo
¥from 25,000 yen, 107-6245)

Imperial Hotel - historic and iconic hotel
(◉ www.imperialhotel.co.jp/e/tokyo ¥from 28,000 yen, 100-8558)

Park Hyatt Tokyo - famous hotel from *Lost In Translation*
(◉ www.tokyo.park.hyatt.com/en/hotel/home.html
¥from 25,000 yen, 163-1055)

Kyoto

Small Luxury Ryugin - high class accommodation in the historic Higashiyama district
(◉ www.kyoto-ryugin.com/english ¥from 30,000 yen, 605-0825)

<u>Hotel Granvia Kyoto</u> - modern rooms adjacent to Kyoto station
(◉ www.granviakyoto.com ¥from 18,000 yen, 600-8216)

Osaka

<u>Imperial Hotel Osaka</u> - quiet inner-city location, not far from the castle
(◉ www.imperialhotel.co.jp/e/osaka ¥from 16,000 yen, 530-0042)

<u>InterContinental Osaka</u> - routinely rated Osaka's best hotel
(◉ www.icosaka.com/en ¥from 20,000 yen, 530-0011)

19. Useful resources

Here are some useful websites for use when planning your trip and during your stay in Japan.

General reference:

www.jnto.go.jp/eng - Japan National Tourist Organization

www.seejapan.co.uk – Great information for planning your trip

www.japan-guide.com – Lots of useful information

www.timeanddate.com/holidays/japan - National holidays

www.jnto.go.jp/sakura/eng/index.php - Cherry blossom bloom forecast

www.jma.go.jp/jma/indexe.html - Weather and natural disasters updates

www.tokyocheapo.com - Full of interesting articles and tips

www.japantoday.com – All the latest national news stories

www.xe.com - Currency exchange rates

Travel:

www.hyperdia.com – Check train times and plan your schedule

www.navitime.co.jp/pcstorage/html/japan_tra vel/english - Travel app

www.japanrailpass.net/en/index.html - JR pass information

www.flypeach.com/pc/en - Budget domestic and international airline

Hotels and accommodation:

www.jalan.net – Japanese hotel booking site

www.expedia.com – Book hotels online

www.booking.com - Book hotels anywhere

www.airbnb.com – Rent a room from local hosts

www.ryokan.or.jp/english - Certified Japanese *ryokans* and hotels

www.japaneseguesthouses.com – Book *ryokan* accommodation online

www.japanican.com/en - Hotels and *ryokan,* easy booking

Food:

www.tabelog.com/en - Find any kind of restaurant

www.gnavi.co.jp/en   - Restaurant listings for all of Japan

www.bento.com - Useful guide to Japanese cuisine

www.happycow.net - Find vegan and vegetarian restaurants

Language:

www.fodors.com/language/japanese - Useful online resource

www.jisho.org - Very useful Japanese-English online dictionary

Outdoors:

www.japanhike.wordpress.com – Guides for various hikes and treks

www.fujisan-climb.jp/en - Mt. Fuji information

www.walkjapan.com - Walking tours combining nature and culture

Internet and Wi-Fi:

www.japan-wireless.com – Popular pocket Wi-Fi rental service

www.japanwifibuddy.com – Friendly and reliable service

www.globaladvancedcomm.com/ pocketwifi.html - A popular provider

Contact the author

Tom Fay has been living and travelling in Japan for a decade, but his journey of discovery continues to this day.
If you have any questions, comments or suggestions for future updates then please don't hesitate to get in touch via his website.
(◙ www.thomasfay.com)

Also feel free to connect on:

Twitter: @T_in_Japan

Instagram: uktoosaka

Was this guidebook useful?

Thank you for buying and reading this guidebook. Word of mouth and personal recommendation are crucial for any author to be successful. So if this book was in any way useful to you, then please consider leaving a review online at
(◙ www.amazon.com). Even if it's only a few words, it would be a great help and hugely appreciated.

Thanks very much for reading, and enjoy your trip to Japan!

64443180R10097

Made in the USA
Middletown, DE
13 February 2018